WINDOWS
— 95 —
VISUAL POCKETGUIDE

VISUAL 3D SERIES

by: maranGraphics' Development Group

Corporate Sales	Canadian Trade Sales
Contact maranGraphics Phone:(905) 890-3300, ext.206 (800) 469-6616, ext.206 Fax: (905) 890-9434	Contact Prentice Hall Canada Phone:(416) 293-3621 (800) 567-3800 Fax: (416) 299-2529

Windows® 95 Visual PocketGuide

Copyright©   1995 by maranGraphics Inc.
                  5755 Coopers Avenue
                  Mississauga, Ontario, Canada
                  L4Z 1R9

Screen shots reprinted with permission from Microsoft Corporation.

Canadian Cataloguing in Publication Data
Maran, Ruth, 1970-
          Windows 95 : pocket guide
(Visual 3-D series)
Includes index.
ISBN 1-896283-07-1

1. Microsoft Windows 95 (Computer file).
2. Operating systems (Computers).
I. MaranGraphics Inc.   II. Title.   III. Series.
QA76.76.063M36 1995   005.4'469   C95-932234-5

Printed in the United States of America

10   9   8   7   6   5   4   3   2   1

Trademark Acknowledgments

maranGraphics Inc. has attempted to include trademark information for products, services and companies referred to in this guide. Although maranGraphics Inc. has made reasonable efforts in gathering this information, it cannot guarantee its accuracy.

Microsoft, MS, MS-DOS, Windows and the Windows logo are either registered trademarks or trademarks of Microsoft Corporation.

Disk Defragmenter, ©1988-1992 Symantec Corporation.

All other brand names and product names used in this book are trademarks, registered trademarks, or trade names of their respective holders. maranGraphics Inc. is not associated with any product or vendor mentioned in this book.

©1995
maranGraphics, Inc.

The animated characters are the
copyright of maranGraphics, Inc.

Every maranGraphics book represents the extraordinary vision and commitment of a unique family:
the Maran family of Toronto, Canada.

Back Row (from left to right): Sherry Maran, Rob Maran, mG,
Richard Maran, Maxine Maran, Jill Maran.
Front Row (from left to right): mG, Judy Maran, Ruth Maran, mG.

Richard Maran is the company founder and its inspirational leader. He began maranGraphics over twenty years ago with a vision of a more efficient way to communicate a visual grammar that fuses text and graphics and allows readers to instantly grasp concepts.

Ruth Maran is the Author and Architect—a role Richard established that now bears Ruth's distinctive touch. She creates the words and visual structure that are the basis for the books.

Judy Maran is Senior Editor. She works with Ruth, Richard, and the highly talented maranGraphics illustrators, designers, and editors to transform Ruth's material into its final form.

Rob Maran is the Technical and Production Specialist. He makes sure the state-of-the-art technology used to create these books always performs as it should.

Sherry Maran manages the Reception, Order Desk, and any number of areas that require immediate attention and a helping hand.

Jill Maran is a jack-of-all-trades and dynamo who fills in anywhere she's needed any time she's back from university.

Maxine Maran is the Business Manager and family sage. She maintains order in the business and family—and keeps everything running smoothly.

Oh, and there's **mG**. He's maranGraphics' spokesperson and, well, star. When you use a maranGraphics book, you'll see a lot of mG and his friends. They're just part of the family!

Credits

Author & Architect:

Ruth Maran

Technical Consultant:

Wendi Blouin Ewbank

Copy Developer & Editor:

Kelleigh Wing

Layout Designers:

David de Haas
Christie Van Duin

Illustrators:

Dave Ross
Tamara Poliquin

Screen Artist:

Andrew Trowbridge

Editors:

Brad Hilderley
Paul Lofthouse
Judy Maran

Post Production:

Robert Maran

Acknowledgments

Thanks to the dedicated staff of maranGraphics, including David de Haas, Francisco Ferreira, Brad Hilderley, Chris K.C. Leung, Paul Lofthouse, Jill Maran, Judy Maran, Maxine Maran, Robert Maran, Sherry Maran, Russ Marini, Neil Mohan, Tamara Poliquin, Dave Ross, Andrew Trowbridge, Christie Van Duin, and Kelleigh Wing.

Thanks also to Saverio C. Tropiano for his assistance and expert advice.

Finally, to Richard Maran who originated the easy-to-use graphic format of this guide. Thank you for your inspiration and guidance.

TABLE OF CONTENTS

GETTING STARTED

WINDOWS BASICS

WORDPAD

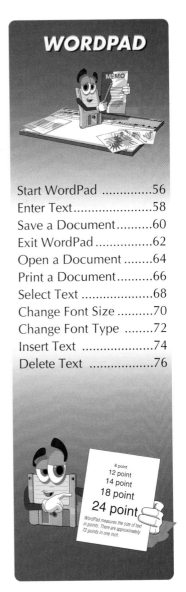

8 point
12 point
14 point
18 point
24 point

WordPad measures the size of text
in points. There are approximately
72 points in one inch.

TABLE OF CONTENTS

PAINT

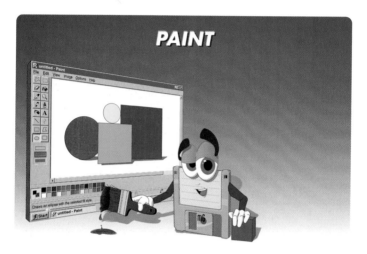

VIEW CONTENTS OF COMPUTER

WORK WITH FILES

TABLE OF CONTENTS

CHANGE WINDOWS SETTINGS

MAINTAIN YOUR COMPUTER

GETTING STARTED

WINDOWS FUNCTIONS

Microsoft® Windows® 95 is a program that controls the overall activity of your computer.

Like an orchestra conductor, Windows ensures that all parts of your computer work together smoothly and efficiently.

CONTROLS YOUR HARDWARE

Windows controls the different parts of your computer system, such as the printer and monitor, and enables them to work together.

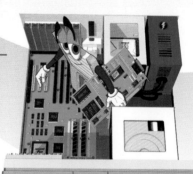

RUNS YOUR PROGRAMS

Windows starts and operates programs, such as Microsoft Word and Lotus 1-2-3. Programs let you write letters, analyze numbers, manage finances, draw pictures and even play games.

Note: Windows comes with several useful programs. These include a word processor (WordPad) and a drawing program (Paint).

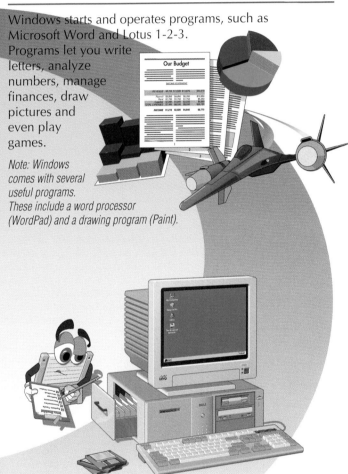

ORGANIZES YOUR INFORMATION

Windows provides ways to organize and manage files stored on your computer. You can use Windows to sort, copy, move, delete and view your files.

THE WINDOWS SCREEN

RECYCLE BIN

Stores all the files you delete and allows you to recover them later.

START BUTTON

Gives you quick access to programs and files.

The Windows screen displays various items. The items that appear depend on how your computer is set up.

MY COMPUTER

Lets you view all the folders and files stored on your computer.

TITLE BAR

Displays the name of an open window.

WINDOW

A rectangle on your screen that displays information.

TASKBAR

Displays the name of each open window on your screen. This lets you easily switch between the open windows.

USING THE MOUSE

USING THE MOUSE

◆ Hold the mouse as shown in the diagram. Use your thumb and two rightmost fingers to move the mouse while your two remaining fingers press the mouse buttons.

The mouse is a hand-held device that lets you select and move items on your screen.

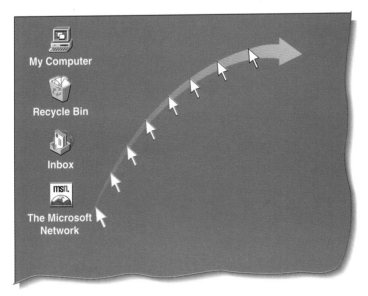

◆ When you move the mouse on your desk, the mouse pointer ⬚ on your screen moves in the same direction. The mouse pointer assumes different shapes (examples: ⬚, I), depending on its location on your screen and the task you are performing.

USING THE MOUSE

PARTS OF THE MOUSE

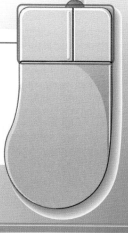

◆ The mouse has a left and right button. You can use these buttons to select commands and choose options.

MOUSE TERMS

CLICK

Press and release the left mouse button.

DOUBLE-CLICK

Quickly press and release the left mouse button twice.

8

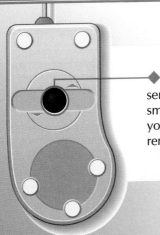

◆ A ball under the mouse senses movement. To ensure smooth motion of the mouse, you should occasionally remove and clean this ball.

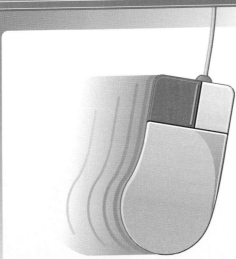

DRAG AND DROP

When the mouse pointer is over an object on your screen, press and hold down the left mouse button. Still holding down the button, move the mouse to where you want to place the object and then release the button.

START WINDOWS

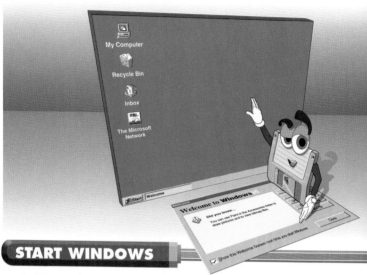

START WINDOWS

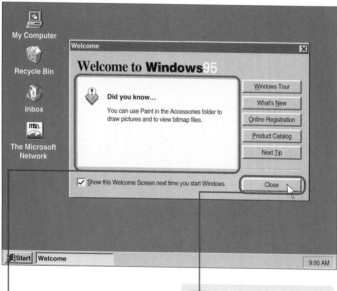

◆ When you start Windows, the **Welcome** dialog box appears. It displays a tip about using Windows.

1 To close the dialog box, move the mouse ⟍ over **Close** and then press the left button.

10

> Windows provides an easy, graphical way for you to use your computer.

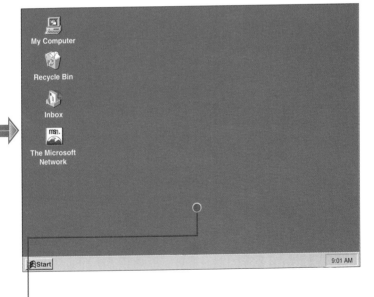

◆ The dialog box disappears and you can clearly view your desktop. The **desktop** is the background area of your screen.

DISPLAY THE DATE

DISPLAY THE DATE

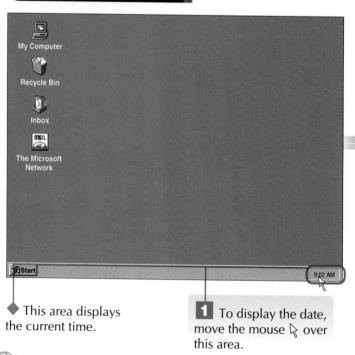

My Computer

Recycle Bin

Inbox

The Microsoft Network

Start

9:02 AM

◆ This area displays the current time.

1 To display the date, move the mouse ↳ over this area.

12

You can easily display the date on your screen.

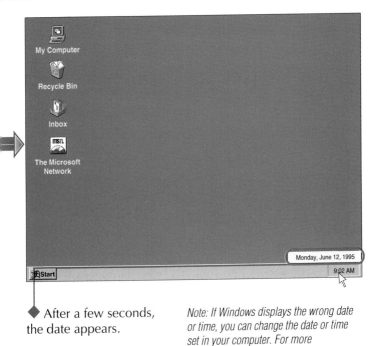

◆ After a few seconds, the date appears.

Note: If Windows displays the wrong date or time, you can change the date or time set in your computer. For more information, refer to page 164.

13

USING THE START BUTTON

USING THE START BUTTON

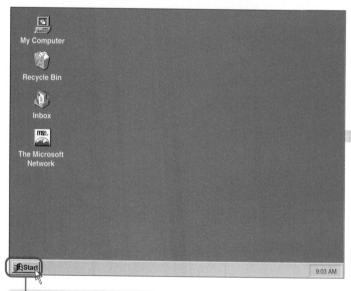

My Computer

Recycle Bin

Inbox

The Microsoft Network

Start   9:03 AM

1 Move the mouse ⟋ over **Start** and then press the left button.

◆ A menu appears.

The Start button lets you display a list of items. You can choose from these items to perform specific tasks in Windows.

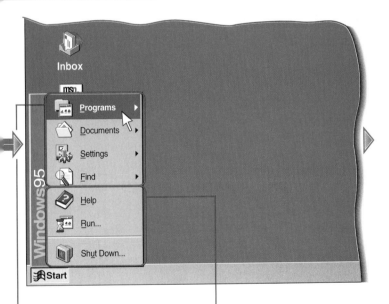

2 To select an item that displays an arrow (▶), move the mouse ⟍ over the item (example: **Programs**). Another menu appears.

◆ To select an item that does not display an arrow, move the mouse ⟍ over the item (example: **Help**) and then press the left button.

CONTINUED

15

USING THE START BUTTON (CONTINUED)

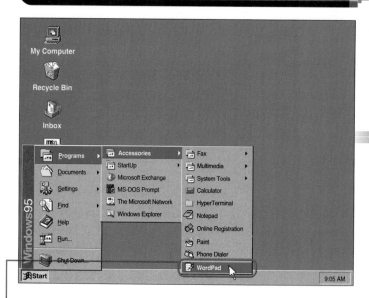

3 Repeat step **2** until you see the item you want to select (example: **WordPad**).

4 Move the mouse ⟍ over the item and then press the left button.

*Note: To close the **Start** menu without selecting an item, move the mouse ⟍ outside the menu area and then press the left button.*

16

Each menu
that appears narrows
your options. This makes
it easier to find the
item you want.

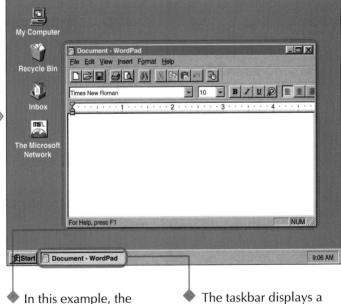

◆ In this example, the
WordPad window appears
on your screen.

Note: For information on using
WordPad, refer to the WordPad
chapter, starting on page 56.

◆ The taskbar displays a
button for the open window.

Note: To close a window to remove it
from your screen, refer to page 42.

17

SHUT DOWN WINDOWS

It's now safe to turn off your computer.

SHUT DOWN WINDOWS

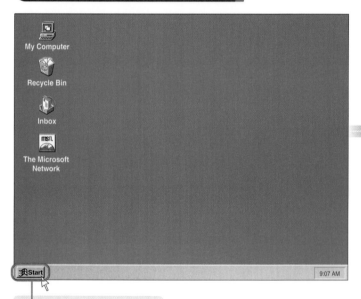

My Computer

Recycle Bin

Inbox

The Microsoft Network

Start

9:07 AM

1 Move the mouse ⍦ over **Start** and then press the left button.

When you finish using Windows, you can shut down the program.

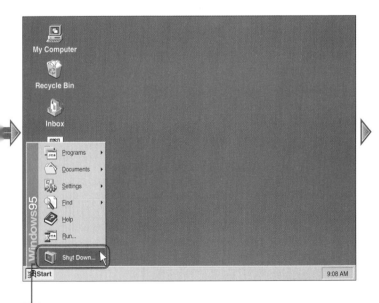

2 Move the mouse over **Shut Down** and then press the left button.

CONTINUED

19

SHUT DOWN WINDOWS (CONTINUED)

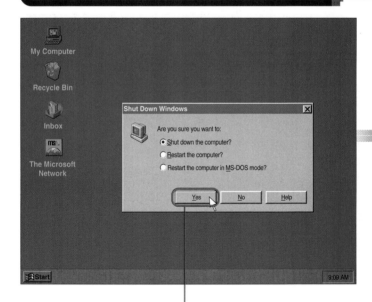

◆ The **Shut Down Windows** dialog box appears.

3 To shut down your computer, move the mouse ⃗ over **Yes** and then press the left button.

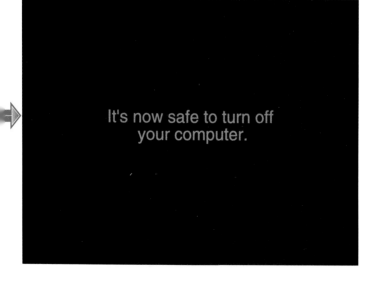

◆ You can now safely
turn off your computer.

WINDOWS BASICS

MAXIMIZE A WINDOW

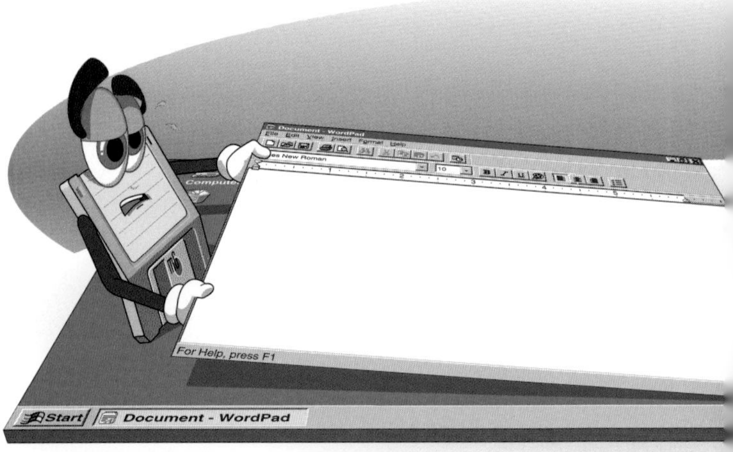

MAXIMIZE A WINDOW

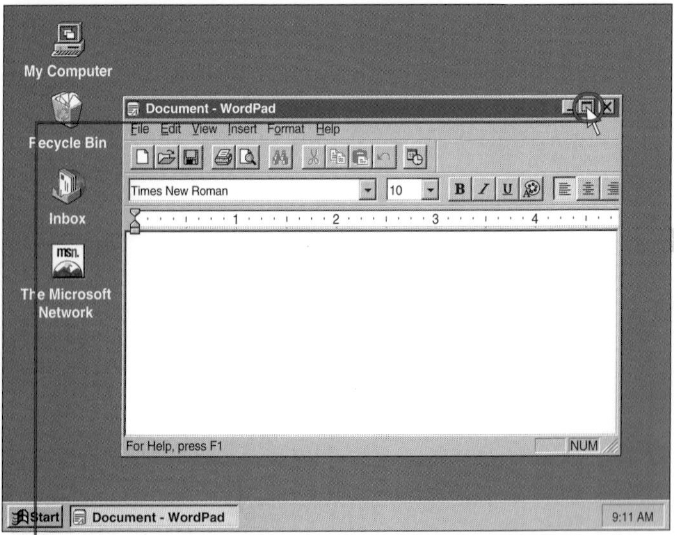

1 Move the mouse over ▣ in the window you want to enlarge and then press the left button.

Note: To display the WordPad window, perform steps 1 to 4 on page 56.

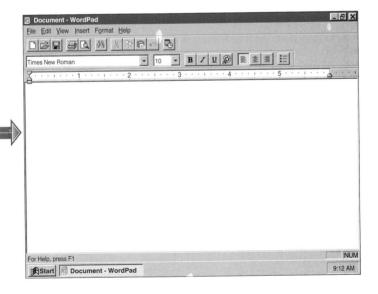

You can enlarge a window to fill your screen. This lets you view more of its contents.

◆ The window fills your screen.

RESTORE A WINDOW

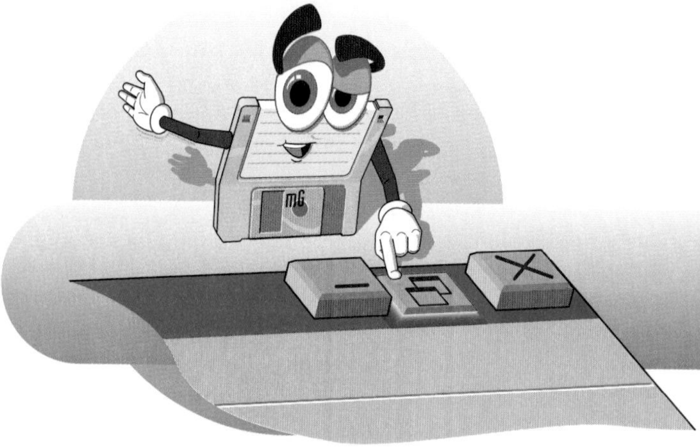

RESTORE A WINDOW

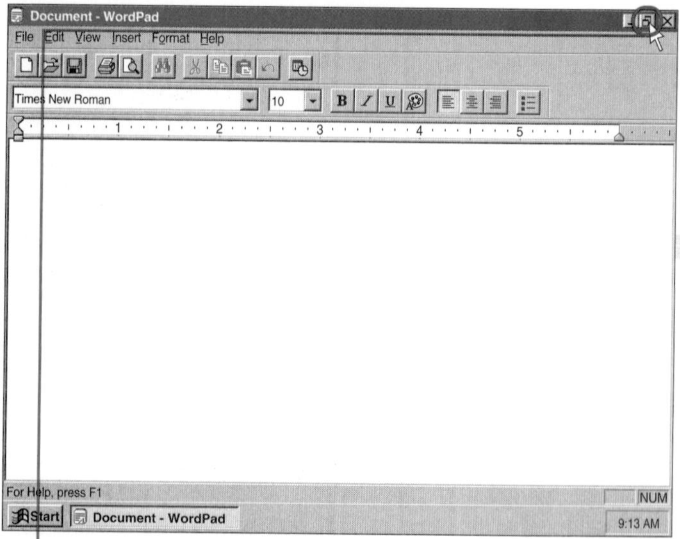

1 Move the mouse over ▣ in the window you want to restore and then press the left button.

Note: Only maximized windows display the Restore button (▣).

You can return a maximized window to its previous size. This lets you view information hidden behind the window.

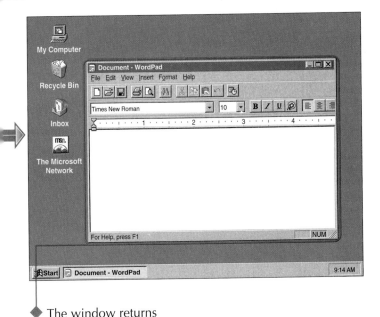

◆ The window returns to its previous size.

MINIMIZE A WINDOW

MINIMIZE A WINDOW

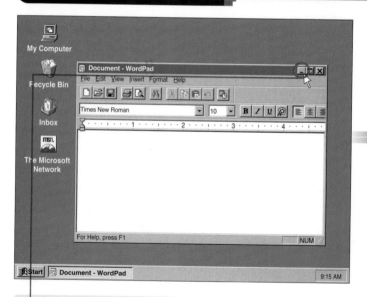

1 Move the mouse ⏳ over ▬ in the window you want to minimize and then press the left button.

28

If you are not using a window, you can minimize the window to remove it from your screen. You can redisplay the window at any time.

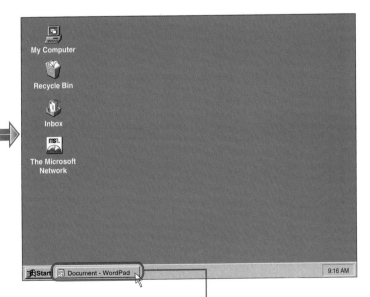

◆ The window disappears.

2 To redisplay the window on your screen, move the mouse over its button on the taskbar and then press the left button.

MOVE A WINDOW

> If a window covers items on your screen, you can move the window to a different location.

MOVE A WINDOW

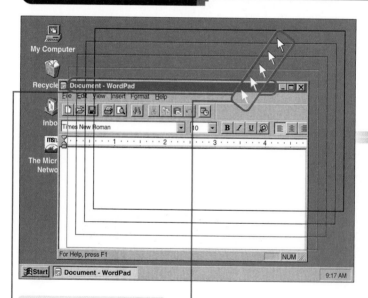

1 Move the mouse ⌖ over the title bar of the window you want to move.

2 Press and hold down the left button as you drag the mouse ⌖ to where you want to place the window.

◆ An outline of the window indicates the new location.

30

3 Release the button and the window moves to the new location.

SIZE A WINDOW

SIZE A WINDOW

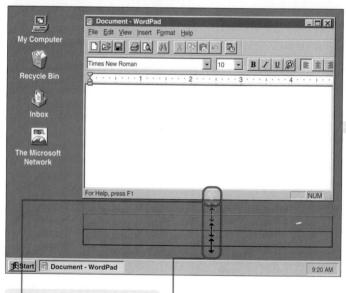

1 Move the mouse ⬚ over an edge of the window you want to size and ⬚ changes to ↕.

2 Press and hold down the left button.

3 Still holding down the button, drag the mouse ↕ until the outline of the window displays the size you want.

32

You can easily change the size of a window displayed on your screen.

- Enlarging a window lets you view more of its contents.

- Reducing a window lets you view items covered by the window.

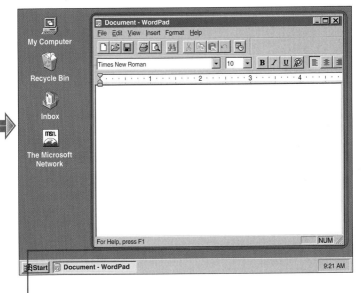

4 Release the button and the window changes to the new size.

Note: You can change the size of a window from any edge or corner.

SWITCH BETWEEN WINDOWS

SWITCH BETWEEN WINDOWS

◆ In this example, the Start button is used to open the **Paint** window.

Note: To use the Start button, refer to page 14.

34

You can have more than one window open at the same time.

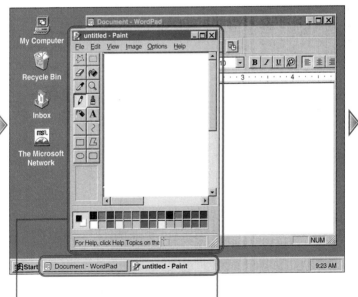

◆ You can only work in one window at a time. The active window (example: **Paint**) appears in front of all other windows.

◆ The taskbar displays a button for each open window on your screen.

CONTINUED

35

SWITCH BETWEEN WINDOWS

SWITCH WINDOWS (CONTINUED)

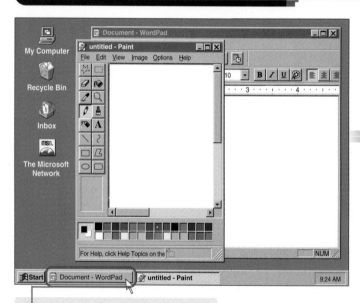

1 To move the window you want to work with to the front, move the mouse ℞ over its button on the taskbar (example: **WordPad**) and then press the left button.

Think of each window as a separate piece of paper. You can rearrange the papers so the one you want to work with is on top.

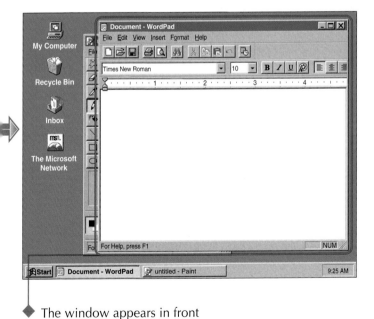

◆ The window appears in front of all other windows.

37

CASCADE WINDOWS

CASCADE WINDOWS

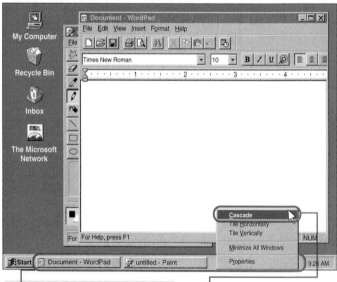

1 Move the mouse ⬡ over an empty area on the taskbar and then press the **right** button. A menu appears.

2 Move the mouse ⬡ over **Cascade** and then press the left button.

38

If you have
several windows open, some
of them may be hidden from
view. The Cascade command
lets you display your open
windows one on top
of the other.

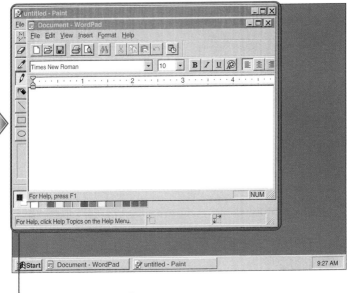

◆ The windows neatly
overlap each other.

TILE WINDOWS

TILE WINDOWS

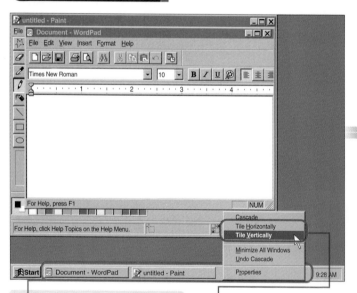

1 Move the mouse ⟍ over an empty area on the taskbar and then press the **right** button. A menu appears.

2 Move the mouse ⟍ over the Tile option you want to use and then press the left button.

You can use the Tile command to view the contents of all your open windows.

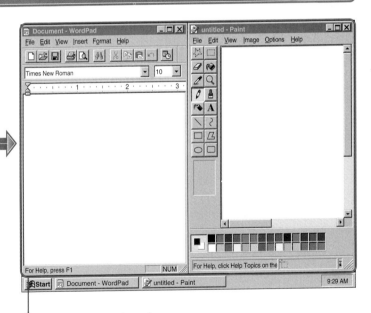

◆ You can now view the contents of all your open windows.

CLOSE A WINDOW

CLOSE A WINDOW

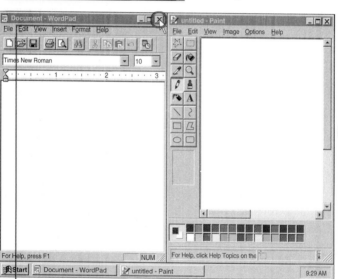

1 Move the mouse ⌖ over ✕ in the window you want to close and then press the left button.

42

When you finish working with a window, you can close the window to remove it from your screen.

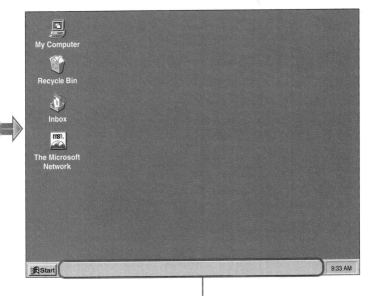

◆ The window disappears from your screen.

◆ The button for the window disappears from the taskbar.

Note: In this example, the Paint window was also closed.

GETTING HELP

GETTING HELP

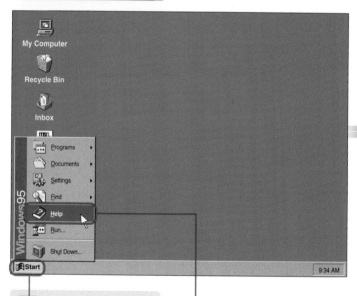

1 Move the mouse ⌖ over **Start** and then press the left button.

2 Move the mouse ⌖ over **Help** and then press the left button.

44

If you do not know how to perform a task, you can use the Help feature to obtain information.

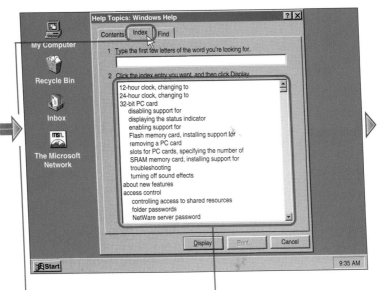

◆ The **Help Topics** window appears.

3 To display the help index, move the mouse ⟡ over the **Index** tab and then press the left button.

◆ This area displays a list of all the available help topics.

CONTINUED

45

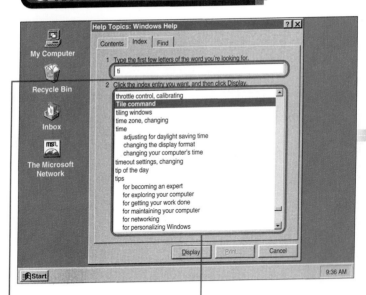

4 Move the mouse I over this area and then press the left button.

5 Type the first few letters of the topic of interest (example: **ti** for **time**).

◆ This area displays topics beginning with the letters you typed.

Note: To browse through the topics, use the scroll bar. For more information, refer to page 50.

The Help feature
can save you time by
eliminating the need
to refer to other
sources.

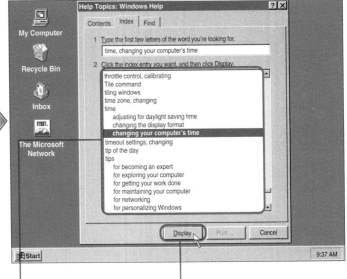

6 Move the mouse ⌖ over the topic you want information on and then press the left button.

7 Move the mouse ⌖ over **Display** and then press the left button.

CONTINUED

47

GETTING HELP

To save you time, the Help feature can open the dialog box that lets you perform the task you want to accomplish.

GETTING HELP (CONTINUED)

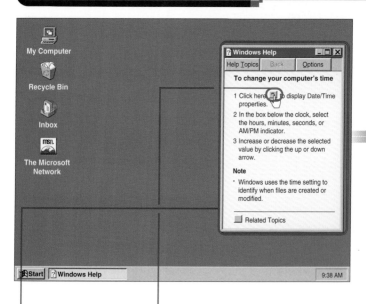

◆ Information on the topic you selected appears.

8 To open the dialog box that lets you perform the task, move the mouse 🖑 over 🔲 and then press the left button.

Note: Some help topics do not display the 🔲 button.

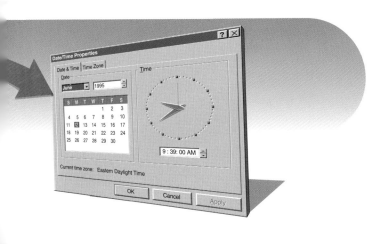

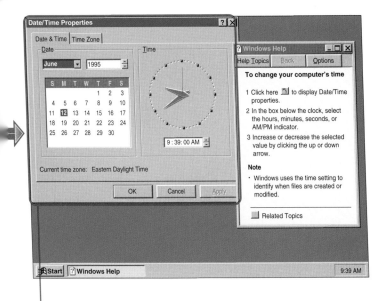

◆ In this example, the **Date/Time Properties** dialog box appears.

Note: To close a window, move the mouse ⌖ over ✕ and then press the left button.

SCROLL THROUGH A WINDOW

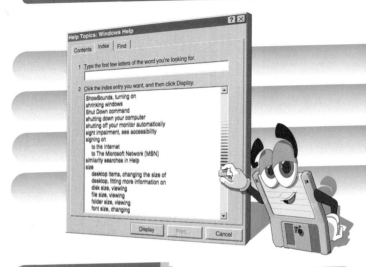

SCROLL DOWN

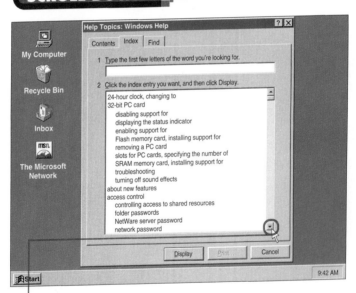

1 Move the mouse ⌖ over ▾ and then press the left button.

◆ The information moves up one line, displaying a new line of information at the bottom of the window.

A scroll bar
lets you browse
through information
in a window.

SCROLL UP

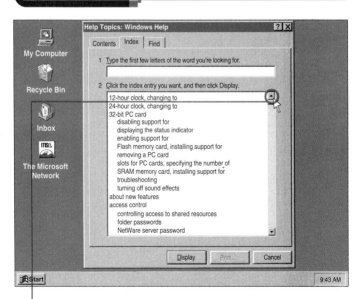

1 Move the mouse ▷
over ▲ and then press
the left button.

◆ The information moves
down one line, displaying
a new line of information
at the top of the window.

51

SCROLL THROUGH A WINDOW

SCROLL TO ANY POSITION

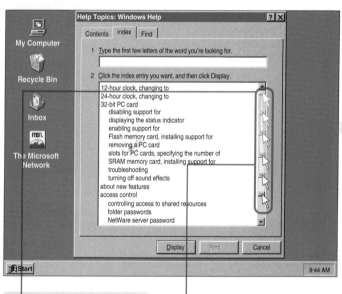

1 Move the mouse ⬡ over the scroll box (▭).

2 Press and hold down the left button as you drag the scroll box along the scroll bar.

You can scroll through a window when the window is not large enough to display all the information it contains.

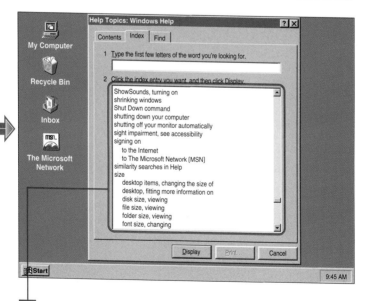

3 Release the button when you see the information you want.

WORDPAD

Start WordPad

Enter Text

Save a Document

Exit WordPad

Open a Document

Print a Document

Select Text

Change Font Size

Change Font Type

Insert Text

Delete Text

8 point
12 point
14 point
18 point
24 point

WordPad measures the size of text in points. There are approximately 72 points in one inch.

START WORDPAD

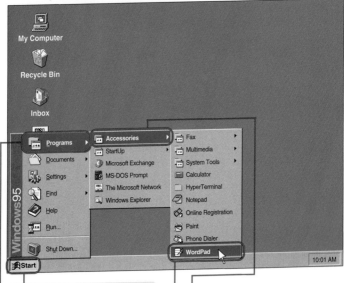

My Computer

Recycle Bin

Inbox

Programs ▶	Accessories ▶	Fax ▶
Documents ▶	StartUp ▶	Multimedia ▶
Settings ▶	Microsoft Exchange	System Tools ▶
Find ▶	MS-DOS Prompt	Calculator
Help	The Microsoft Network	HyperTerminal
Run...	Windows Explorer	Notepad
Shut Down...		Online Registration
		Paint
		Phone Dialer
		WordPad

Windows95

Start

10:01 AM

1 Move the mouse ⌖ over **Start** and then press the left button.

2 Move the mouse ⌖ over **Programs**.

3 Move the mouse ⌖ over **Accessories**.

4 Move the mouse ⌖ over **WordPad** and then press the left button.

WordPad helps you create professional-looking documents, such as letters and memos.

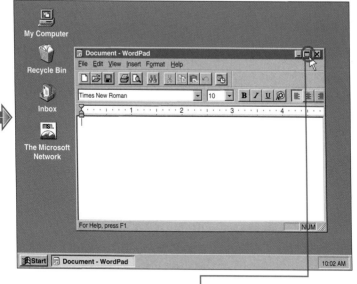

◆ The **WordPad** window appears.

5 To enlarge the **WordPad** window to fill your screen, move the mouse ⍨ over 🔲 and then press the left button.

57

ENTER TEXT

ENTER TEXT

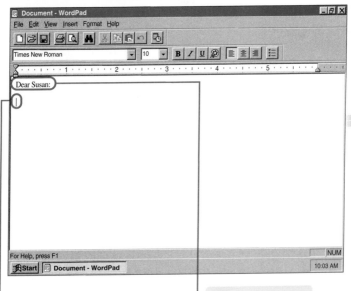

◆ The flashing line in the window is called the insertion point. It indicates where the text you type will appear.

1 Type the first line of text.

2 To start a new paragraph, press **Enter** twice.

When typing text in a document, you do not need to press **Enter** at the end of a line. WordPad automatically moves the text to the next line.

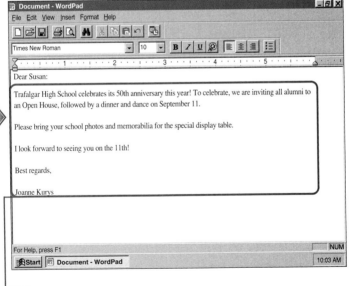

3 Type the remaining text.

◆ Press **Enter** only when you want to start a new line or paragraph.

SAVE A DOCUMENT

SAVE A DOCUMENT

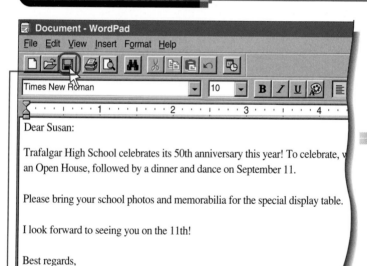

Document - WordPad

File Edit View Insert Format Help

Times New Roman   ▼   10   ▼   **B** *I* U

Dear Susan:

Trafalgar High School celebrates its 50th anniversary this year! To celebrate, an Open House, followed by a dinner and dance on September 11.

Please bring your school photos and memorabilia for the special display table.

I look forward to seeing you on the 11th!

Best regards,

1 Move the mouse ⌖ over 🖫 and then press the left button.

◆ The **Save As** dialog box appears.

*Note: If you previously saved your document, the **Save As** dialog box will not appear, since you have already named the document.*

60

You should save your document to store it for future use. This lets you later retrieve the document for reviewing or editing purposes.

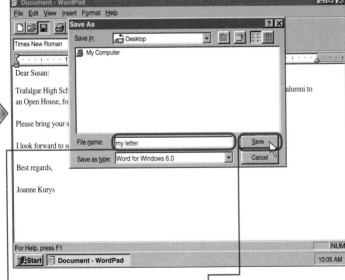

2 Type a name for your document (example: **my letter**).

*Note: You can use up to 255 characters to name a document. The name cannot contain the characters \ ? : * " < > or |.*

3 Move the mouse ⌖ over **Save** and then press the left button.

*Note: To avoid losing your work, you should save your document every 5 to 10 minutes. To do so, repeat step **1**.*

EXIT WORDPAD

EXIT WORDPAD

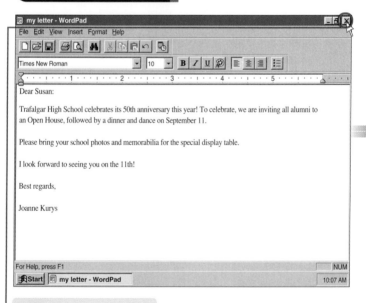

1 Move the mouse ▷ over **X** and then press the left button.

When you finish using WordPad, you can exit the program.

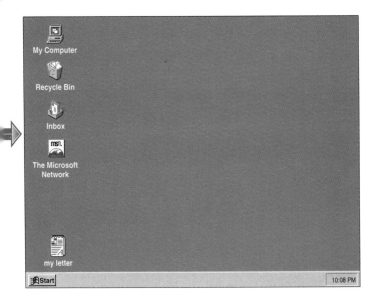

◆ The WordPad window disappears from your screen.

Note: To restart WordPad, refer to page 56.

OPEN A DOCUMENT

OPEN A DOCUMENT

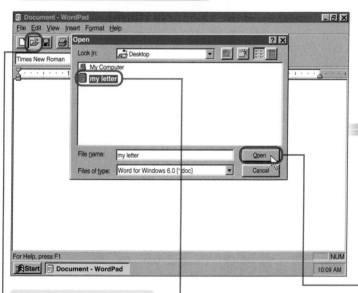

1 Move the mouse ⬚ over ⬚ and then press the left button.

◆ The **Open** dialog box appears.

2 Move the mouse ⬚ over the name of the document you want to open and then press the left button.

Note: If you cannot find the document you want to open, refer to page 156 to find the document.

64

You can open
a saved document and
display it on your screen.
This lets you view and
make changes to the
document.

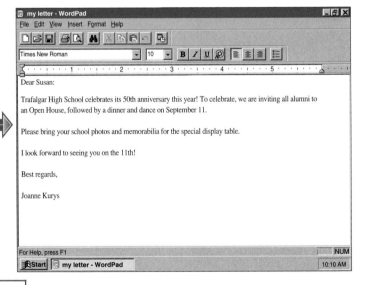

3 Move the mouse 👆
over **Open** and then press
the left button.

◆ WordPad opens the
document and displays it
on your screen. You can
now review and make
changes to the document.

PRINT A DOCUMENT

PRINT A DOCUMENT

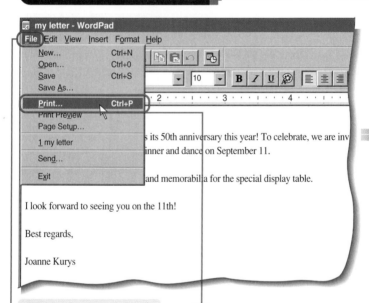

my letter - WordPad

File | Edit | View | Insert | Format | Help

New...	Ctrl+N
Open...	Ctrl+O
Save	Ctrl+S
Save As...	
Print...	Ctrl+P
Print Preview	
Page Setup...	
1 my letter	
Send...	
Exit	

Dear Susan,

Trafalgar High School celebrates its 50th anniversary this year! To celebrate, we are inv

an Open House, followed by a dinner and dance on September 11.

Please bring your school photos and memorabilia for the special display table.

I look forward to seeing you on the 11th!

Best regards,

Joanne Kurys

1 Move the mouse ⌖ over **File** and then press the left button.

2 Move the mouse ⌖ over **Print** and then press the left button.

66

You can produce a paper copy of the document displayed on your screen.

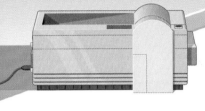

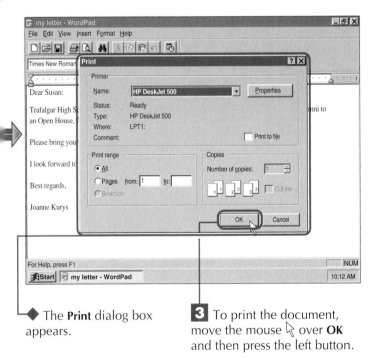

◆ The **Print** dialog box appears.

3 To print the document, move the mouse ⌖ over **OK** and then press the left button.

SELECT TEXT

school photos and memorabilia

SELECT TEXT

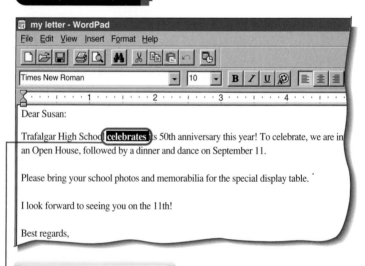

| my letter - WordPad |

File   Edit   View   Insert   Format   Help

Times New Roman   10   **B** *I* U

Dear Susan:

Trafalgar High School **celebrates** its 50th anniversary this year! To celebrate, we are in
an Open House, followed by a dinner and dance on September 11.

Please bring your school photos and memorabilia for the special display table.

I look forward to seeing you on the 11th!

Best regards,

SELECT A WORD

1 Move the mouse I
anywhere over the word
you want to select and
then quickly press the left
button twice.

◆ To cancel a text
selection, move the
mouse I outside the
selected area and then
press the left button.

Before performing a task, you must first select the text you want to work with. Selected text appears highlighted on your screen.

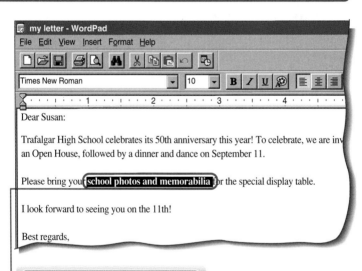

SELECT ANY AMOUNT OF TEXT

1 Move the mouse I over the first word you want to select.

2 Press and hold down the left button as you drag the mouse ⌖ over the text you want to select. Then release the button.

Note: To quickly select all the text in your document, press **Ctrl** + **A**.

CHANGE FONT SIZE

8 point
12 point
14 point
18 point
24 point

WordPad measures the size of text in points. There are approximately 72 points in one inch.

CHANGE FONT SIZE

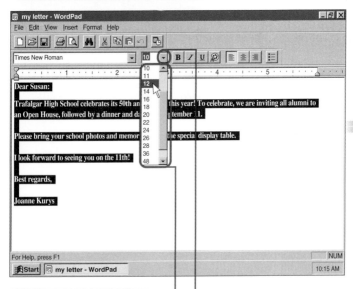

1 Select the text you want to make larger or smaller.

Note: To select text, refer to page 68.

2 Move the mouse ⌖ over ⏷ in the **Font Size** box and then press the left button.

3 Move the mouse ⌖ over the size you want to use (example: **12**) and then press the left button.

You can increase or decrease the size of text in your document.

- Larger text is easier to read.

- Smaller text lets you fit more information on one page.

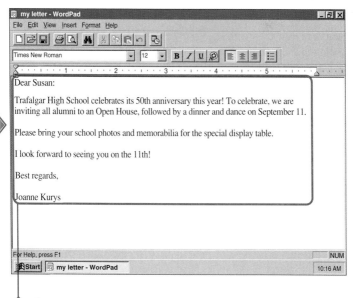

◆ The text you selected changes to the new size.

Note: To deselect text, move the mouse I outside the selected area and then press the left button.

CHANGE FONT TYPE

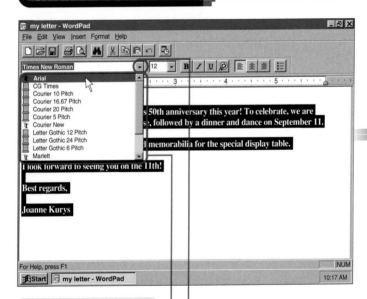

1 Select the text you want to change.

Note: To select text, refer to page 68.

2 Move the mouse ⌖ over ▾ in the **Font** box and then press the left button.

3 Move the mouse ⌖ over the font type you want to use (example: **Arial**) and then press the left button.

You can enhance the appearance of your document by changing the design of characters.

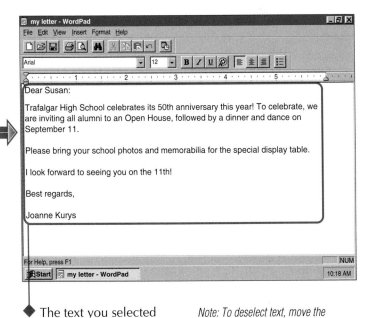

◆ The text you selected changes to the new font type.

Note: To deselect text, move the mouse I outside the selected area and then press the left button.

INSERT TEXT

You can easily add new text to your document.

INSERT TEXT

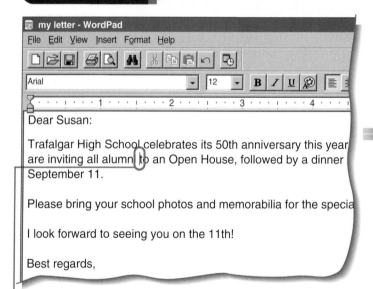

my letter - WordPad

File Edit View Insert Format Help

Arial   12   **B** *I* U

Dear Susan:

Trafalgar High School celebrates its 50th anniversary this year
are inviting all alumni to an Open House, followed by a dinner
September 11.

Please bring your school photos and memorabilia for the specia

I look forward to seeing you on the 11th!

Best regards,

1 Move the mouse I to
where you want to insert
the new text and then
press the left button.

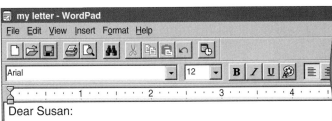

my letter - WordPad

File Edit View Insert Format Help

Arial   12   **B** *I* U

Dear Susan:

Trafalgar High School celebrates its 50th anniversary this year!
are inviting all alumni and students to an Open House, followed
dance on September 11.

Please bring your school photos and memorabilia for the specia

I look forward to seeing you on the 11th!

Best regards,

2 Type the text you want
to insert.

*Note: The words to the right of
the new text move forward.*

3 To insert a blank space,
press the **Spacebar**.

75

DELETE TEXT

DELETE TEXT

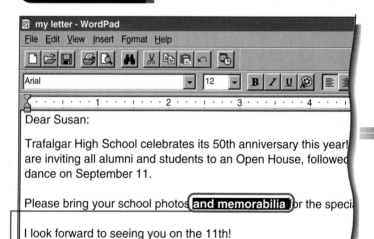

1 Select the text you want to delete.

Note: To select text, refer to page 68.

> You can easily
> remove text you no
> longer need.

my letter - WordPad

File Edit View Insert Format Help

Arial 12 B I U

Dear Susan:

Trafalgar High School celebrates its 50th anniversary this year!
are inviting all alumni and students to an Open House, followed
dance on September 11.

Please bring your school photos for the special display table.

I look forward to seeing you on the 11th!

Best regards,

2 Press Delete on your
keyboard to remove
the text.

PAINT

- Start Paint
- Draw Lines
- Draw Shapes
- Erase an Area
- Undo Last Change
- Save a Drawing
- Exit Paint
- Open a Drawing

START PAINT

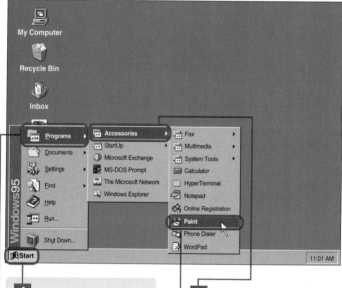

1 Move the mouse ⍿ over **Start** and then press the left button.

2 Move the mouse ⍿ over **Programs**.

3 Move the mouse ⍿ over **Accessories**.

4 Move the mouse ⍿ over **Paint** and then press the left button.

80

Paint lets
you use your artistic
abilities to draw pictures
and maps on your
computer.

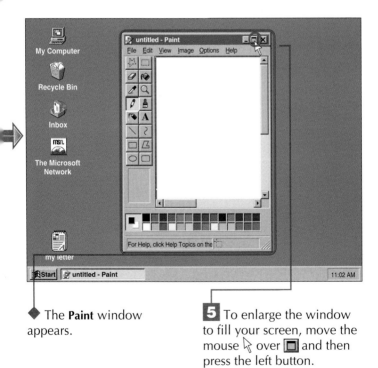

◆ The **Paint** window
appears.

5 To enlarge the window
to fill your screen, move the
mouse ▷ over ▢ and then
press the left button.

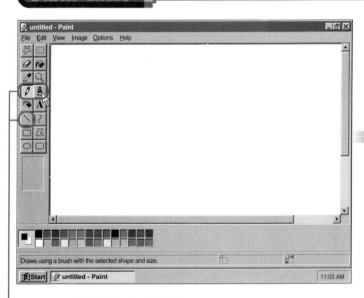

DRAW LINES

1 Move the mouse ↳ over the line tool you want to use (example: 🖌) and then press the left button.

✏	Draws thin, wavy lines.
🖌	Draws wavy lines of different thicknesses.
╲	Draws straight lines of different thicknesses.

82

You can draw straight or wavy lines in any color displayed at the bottom of your screen.

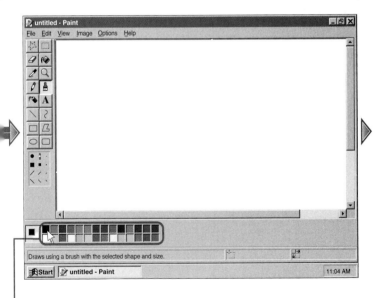

CONTINUED

2 To select a color for the line, move the mouse ▷ over the color (example: ■) and then press the left button.

DRAW LINES

You can select a different thickness for your line.

DRAW LINES (CONTINUED)

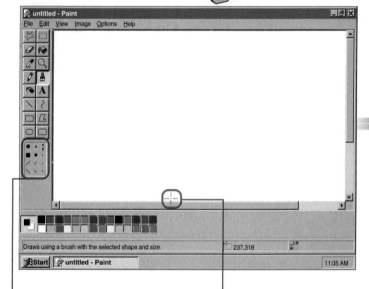

3 To select a line thickness, move the mouse ⬚ over one of these options and then press the left button.

Note: The ✏ tool does not provide any line thickness options.

4 Move the mouse ⬚ to where you want to begin drawing the line and ⬚ changes to -¦- or ✏.

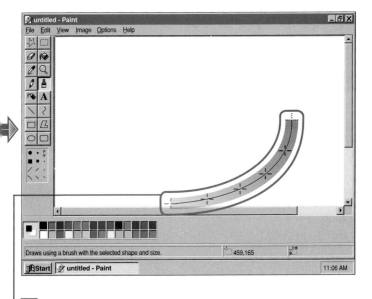

5 Press and hold down the left button as you move the mouse -|- until the line is the length you want. Then release the button.

Note: When using the ＼ or ✏ tool, you can draw a perfectly horizontal, vertical or 45-degree line. To do so, press and hold down **Shift** *before and during step* **5**.

85

DRAW SHAPES

Paint offers these options for creating shapes.

DRAW SHAPES

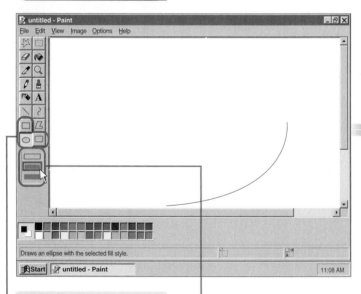

Draws an ellipse with the selected fill style.

1 Move the mouse ⯈ over the tool displaying the shape you want to draw (example: ⬭) and then press the left button.

2 To select how you want the shape to appear, move the mouse ⯈ over one of these options and then press the left button.

Note: For more information, refer to the top of page 87.

86

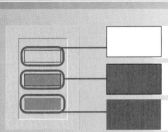

Draws the outline of a shape.

Draws the outline of a shape and fills the inside with color.

Draws a colored shape with no outline.

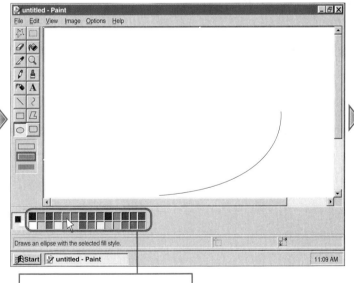

3 To select a color for the outline of the shape, move the mouse ⌖ over the color (example: ■) and then press the left button.

4 To select a color for the inside of the shape, move the mouse ⌖ over the color (example: ■) and then press the **right** button.

CONTINUED

87

DRAW SHAPES

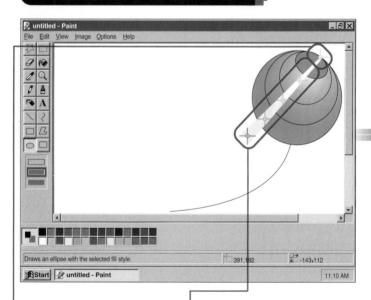

5 Move the mouse ⬚ to where you want to begin drawing the shape and ⬚ changes to ╋.

6 Press and hold down the left button as you drag the shape to the size you want. Then release the button.

Note: To draw a perfect circle or square, press and hold down **Shift** *before and during step* **6** .

88

You can
draw circles and
squares to complete
your drawing.

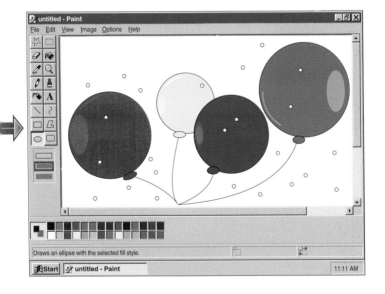

◆ You can now use the
shape and line tools to
complete your drawing.

*Note: For information on drawing
lines, refer to page 82.*

*Note: To print the drawing, perform
steps 1 to 3 starting on page 66.*

ERASE AN AREA

ERASE AN AREA

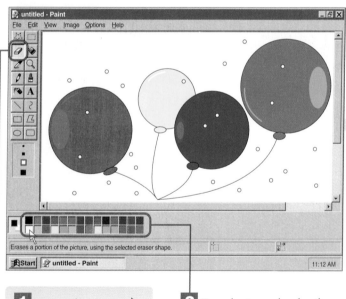

1 Move the mouse ⬚ over 🖉 and then press the left button.

2 To select a color for the eraser, move the mouse ⬚ over the color (example: ☐) and then press the **right** button.

You can use the Eraser tool to remove part of your drawing.

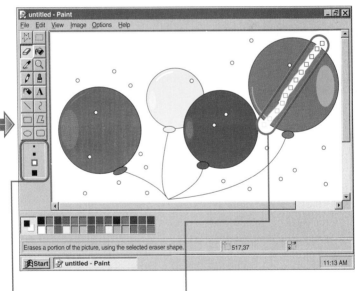

Erases a portion of the picture, using the selected eraser shape.

3 Move the mouse ⬡ over the eraser size you want to use and then press the left button.

4 Move the mouse ⬡ to where you want to start erasing (⬡ changes to □).

5 Press and hold down the left button as you move the mouse □ over the area you want to erase. Then release the button.

91

UNDO LAST CHANGE

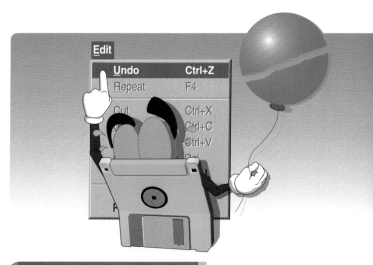

UNDO LAST CHANGE

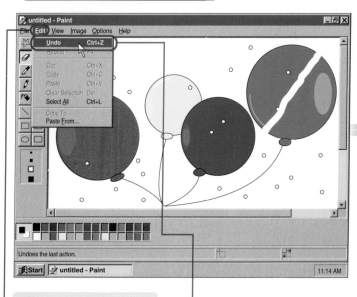

1 Move the mouse ⤢ over **Edit** and then press the left button.

2 Move the mouse ⤢ over **Undo** and then press the left button.

Paint remembers the last change you made to your drawing. If you regret this change, you can cancel it by using the Undo feature.

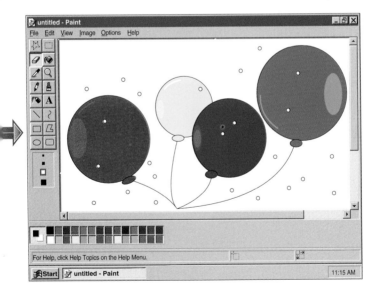

◆ Paint cancels the last change you made to the drawing.

93

SAVE A DRAWING

SAVE A DRAWING

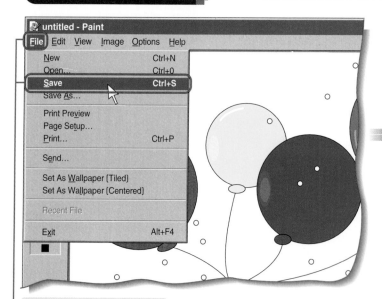

1 Move the mouse ⤢ over **File** and then press the left button.

2 Move the mouse ⤢ over **Save** and then press the left button.

◆ The **Save As** dialog box appears.

*Note: If you previously saved your drawing, the **Save As** dialog box will not appear, since you have already named the drawing.*

94

You should save
your drawing to store it for
future use. This lets you later
review and make changes
to the drawing.

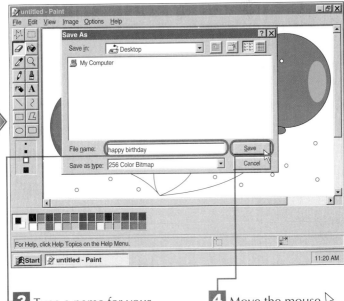

3 Type a name for your drawing.

*Note: You can use up to 255 characters to name your drawing. The name cannot contain the characters \ ? : * " < > or |.*

4 Move the mouse ⌖ over **Save** and then press the left button.

Note: To avoid losing your work, you should save your drawing every 5 to 10 minutes. To do so, repeat steps 1 and 2.

EXIT PAINT

When you finish using Paint, you can exit the program.

EXIT PAINT

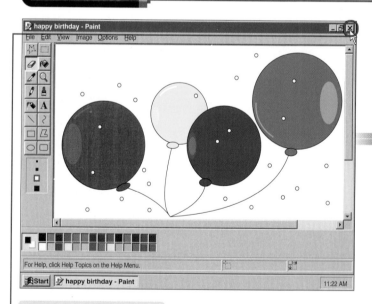

1 Move the mouse ⌖ over ✕ and then press the left button.

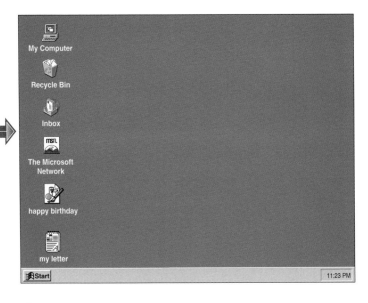

◆ The Paint window disappears from your screen.

Note: To restart Paint, refer to page 80.

OPEN A DRAWING

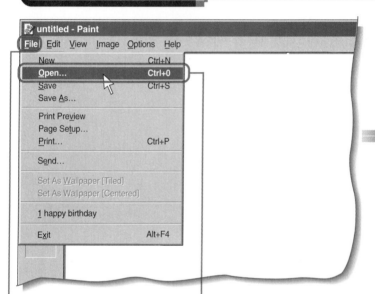

◆ To start **Paint**, refer to page 80.

1 Move the mouse ⬎ over **File** and then press the left button.

2 Move the mouse ⬎ over **Open** and then press the left button.

◆ The **Open** dialog box appears.

98

You can open a saved drawing and display it on your screen.

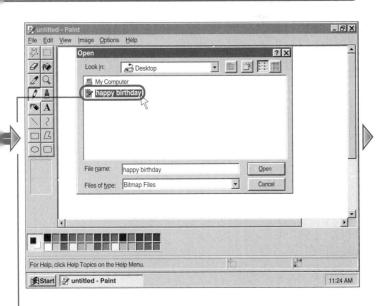

3 Move the mouse ⯈ over the name of the drawing you want to open and then press the left button.

Note: If you cannot find the drawing you want to open, refer to page 156 to find the drawing.

OPEN A DRAWING

OPEN A DRAWING (CONTINUED)

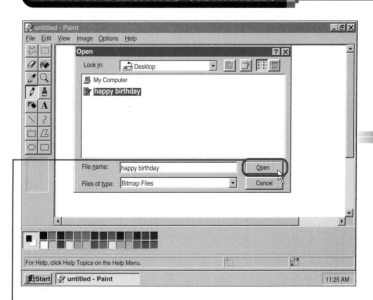

4 Move the mouse ⊹ over **Open** and then press the left button.

After opening a drawing, you can view and make changes to the drawing.

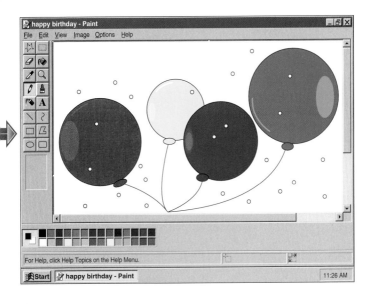

◆ Paint opens the drawing and displays it on your screen. You can now review and make changes to the drawing.

101

VIEW CONTENTS OF COMPUTER

The hard drive is the primary device that a computer uses to store information.

Most computers come with one hard drive, located inside the computer case. It is called drive C.

FLOPPY DRIVE (A:)

A floppy drive stores and retrieves information on floppy disks (diskettes). If your computer has only one floppy drive, it is called drive A. If your computer has two floppy drives, the second drive is called drive B.

CD-ROM DRIVE (D:)

A CD-ROM drive is a device that reads information stored on compact discs. You cannot change information stored on a compact disc.

Note: Your computer may not have a CD-ROM drive.

VIEW CONTENTS OF COMPUTER

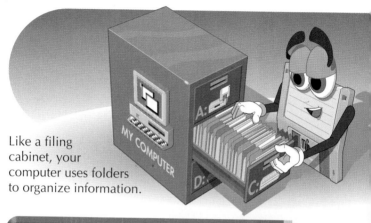

Like a filing cabinet, your computer uses folders to organize information.

VIEW CONTENTS OF COMPUTER

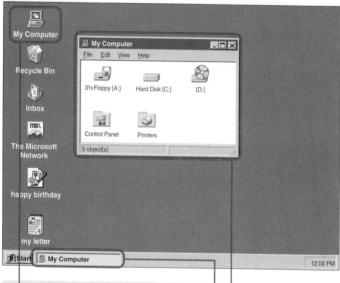

1 To view the contents of your computer, move the mouse ⟍ over **My Computer** and then quickly press the left button twice.

◆ The **My Computer** window opens.

◆ The taskbar displays the name of the opened window.

You can easily view the folders and files stored on your computer.

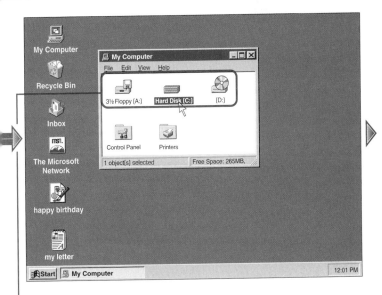

◆ These objects represent the drives on your computer.

2 To display the contents of a drive, move the mouse ⊾ over the drive (example: **C:**) and then quickly press the left button twice.

*Note: If you want to view the contents of a floppy or CD-ROM drive, make sure you insert a floppy disk or CD-ROM disc before performing step **2**.*

CONTINUED

A window on your screen can display folders and files.

VIEW CONTENTS (CONTINUED)

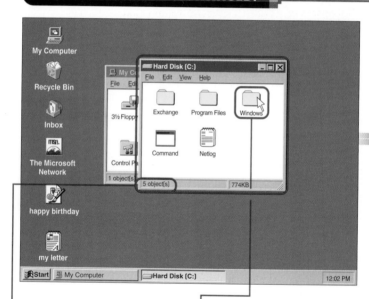

◆ A window appears, displaying the contents of the drive.

◆ This area tells you how many objects are in the window.

3 To display the contents of a folder, move the mouse ⌖ over the folder (example: **Windows**) and then quickly press the left button twice.

108

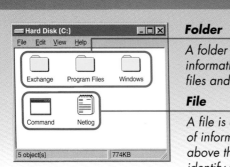

Folder

A folder stores related information. It can contain files and other folders.

File

A file is a named collection of information. The picture above the file name helps identify the file type.

◆ A new window appears, displaying the contents of the folder.

CHANGE SIZE OF ITEMS

CHANGE SIZE OF ITEMS

1 Move the mouse ↖ over **View** and then press the left button.

2 To enlarge the items in a window, move the mouse ↖ over **Large Icons** and then press the left button.

You can change the size of items displayed in a window. Enlarging items lets you view the items more clearly.

◆ The items change to a larger size.

Note: To return to the smaller item size, repeat steps 1 and 2, selecting Small Icons in step 2.

ARRANGE ITEMS

You can have Windows automatically arrange items to fit in a window.

ARRANGE ITEMS

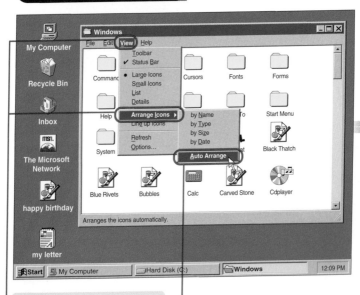

1 Move the mouse ↕ over **View** and then press the left button.

2 Move the mouse ↕ over **Arrange Icons**.

3 To turn on Auto Arrange, move the mouse ↕ over **Auto Arrange** and then press the left button.

Note: If this area displays a check mark (✔), Auto Arrange is on. To leave the feature on, press Alt on your keyboard.

If you change the size of a window when the Auto Arrange feature is on, Windows will automatically rearrange the items to fit the new size.

◆ The items fit in the window.

◆ To turn off Auto Arrange, repeat steps **1** to **3**.

113

DISPLAY FILE INFORMATION

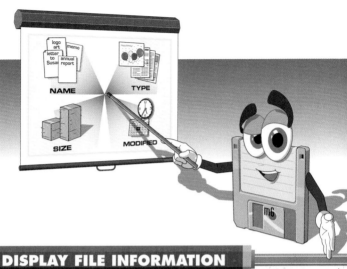

DISPLAY FILE INFORMATION

1 Move the mouse ↘ over **View** and then press the left button.

2 Move the mouse ↘ over **Details** and then press the left button.

Windows
lets you display
information about
the files listed in
a window.

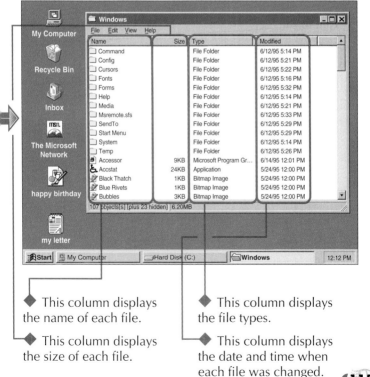

◆ This column displays
the name of each file.

◆ This column displays
the size of each file.

◆ This column displays
the file types.

◆ This column displays
the date and time when
each file was changed.

DISPLAY FILE NAMES ONLY

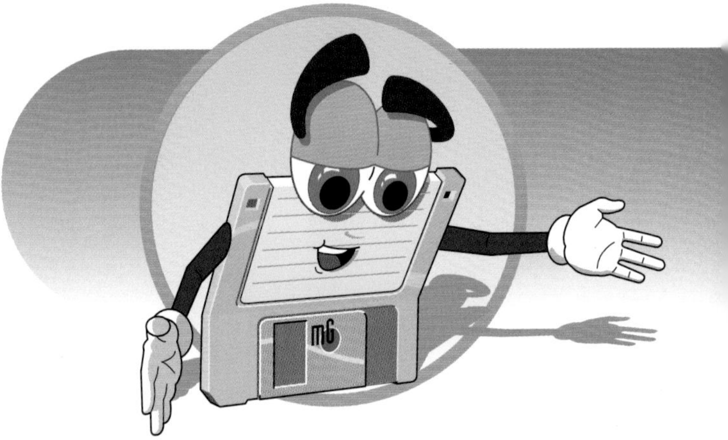

DISPLAY FILE NAMES ONLY

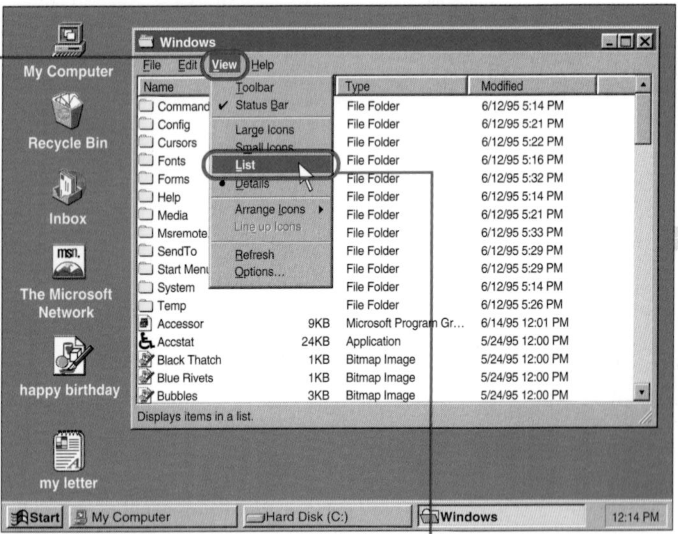

1 To hide the file information and display only the file names, move the mouse over **View** and then press the left button.

2 Move the mouse over **List** and then press the left button.

You can hide
the file information
and display only
the file names.

◆ Only the file names are
displayed on your screen.

SORT ITEMS

SORT BY NAME

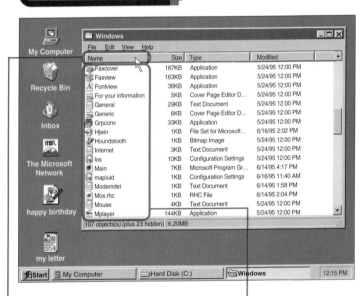

1 To sort the item names from A to Z, move the mouse ⬚ over **Name** and then press the left button.

*Note: If the **Name** button is not displayed, perform steps **1** and **2** on page 114.*

◆ The items in the window are sorted.

*Note: To sort the item names from Z to A, repeat step **1**.*

You can
sort the items
displayed in a window
by name or size.

SORT BY SIZE

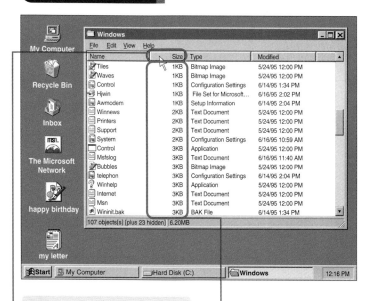

1 To sort the items from smallest to largest, move the mouse ⍟ over **Size** and then press the left button.

*Note: If the **Size** button is not displayed, perform steps **1** and **2** on page 114.*

◆ The items in the window are sorted.

*Note: To sort the items from largest to smallest, repeat step **1**.*

119

SORT ITEMS

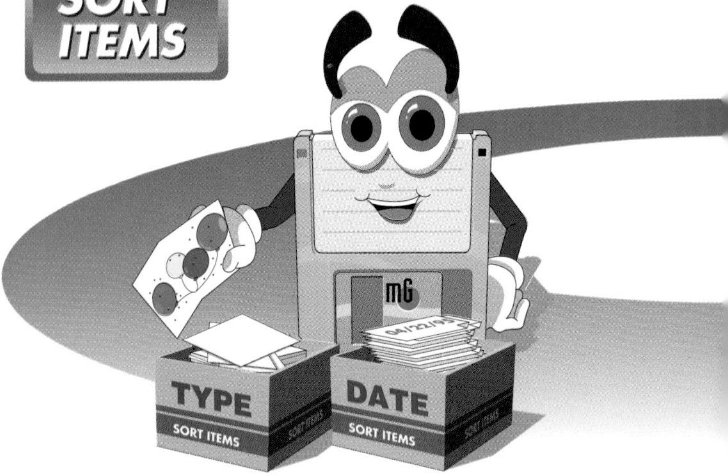

SORT BY TYPE

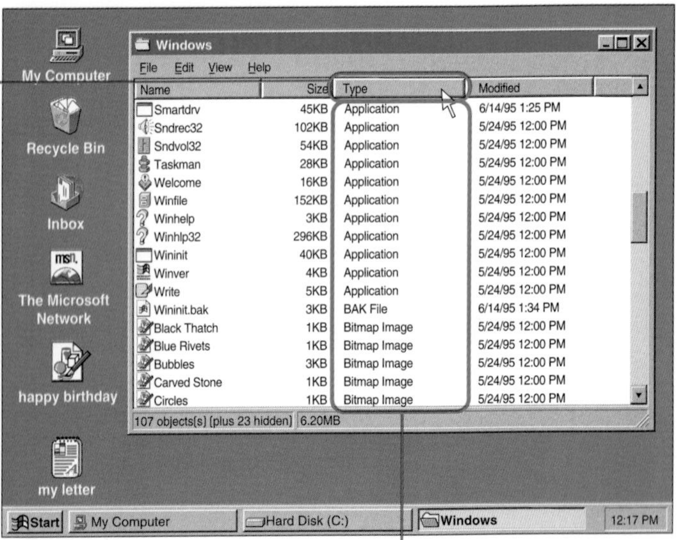

1 To sort the item types from A to Z, move the mouse ↖ over **Type** and then press the left button.

*Note: If the **Type** button is not displayed, perform steps **1** and **2** on page 114.*

◆ The items in the window are sorted.

*Note: To sort the item types from Z to A, repeat step **1**.*

You can also
sort the items
displayed in a window
by type or date.

SORT BY DATE

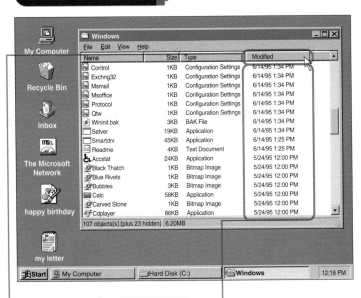

1 To sort the items from newest to oldest, move the mouse ⤹ over **Modified** and then press the left button.

*Note: If the **Modified** button is not displayed, perform steps **1** and **2** on page 114.*

◆ The items in the window are sorted.

*Note: To sort the items from oldest to newest, repeat step **1**.*

In this chapter you will learn how to work with files stored on your computer.

WORK WITH FILES

Select Files

Create a New Folder

Move a File to a Folder

Copy a File to a Floppy Disk

Rename a File

Open a File

Open a Recently Used File

Print a File

Delete a File

Restore a Deleted File

Find a File

SELECT FILES

SELECT A FILE

1 Move the mouse ⬚ over the file you want to select and then press the left button.

◆ The file is highlighted.

Note: To deselect files, move the mouse ⬚ over a blank area in the window and then press the left button.

124

Before working
with a file, you must
select the file you want to
work with. Selected files
appear highlighted
on your screen.

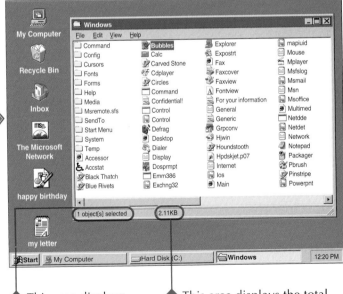

◆ This area displays
the number of files
you selected.

◆ This area displays the total
size of the files you selected.

*Note: One byte equals one character. One
kilobyte (KB) equals approximately one
page of double spaced text.*

SELECT FILES

SELECT A GROUP OF FILES

1 Move the mouse ⬚ over the first file you want to select and then press the left button.

2 Press and hold down Shift on your keyboard.

3 Still holding down Shift, move the mouse ⬚ over the last file you want to select and then press the left button.

Windows lets you easily select multiple files. This lets you work with several files at the same time.

SELECT ANY FILES

1 Move the mouse ⇖ over a file you want to select and then press the left button.

2 Press and hold down `Ctrl` on your keyboard.

3 Still holding down `Ctrl`, repeat step **1** for each file you want to select.

127

CREATE A NEW FOLDER

CREATE A NEW FOLDER

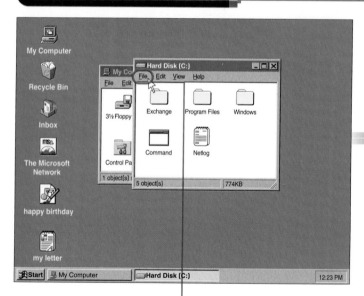

1 Display the contents of the drive or folder where you want to place the new folder.

Note: For more information, refer to page 106.

2 To deselect any selected files, move the mouse ⇖ over a blank area in the window and then press the left button.

3 Move the mouse ⇖ over **File** and then press the left button.

You can create a new folder to better organize the information stored on your computer.

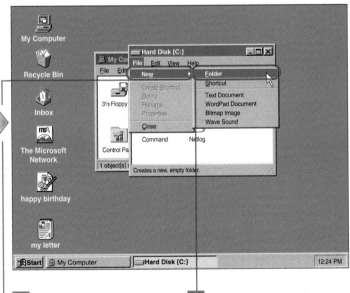

4 Move the mouse ⌕ over **New**.

5 Move the mouse ⌕ over **Folder** and then press the left button.

CONTINUED

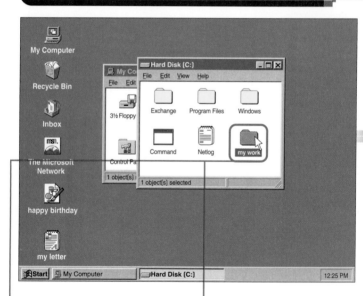

◆ The new folder appears, displaying a temporary name (New Folder).

6 Type a name for the new folder (example: **my work**) and then press Enter .

7 To display the contents of the new folder, move the mouse ⬚ over the folder and then quickly press the left button twice.

Creating
a folder is like
placing a new folder
in a filing cabinet.

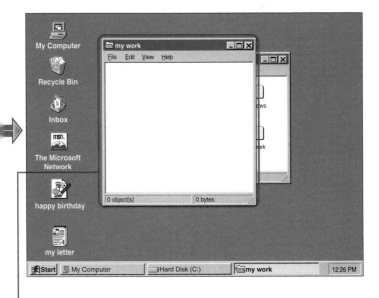

◆ The contents of
the folder appear.

*Note: To close a window, move the
mouse ⬛ over ☒ and then press
the left button.*

131

MOVE A FILE TO A FOLDER

MOVE A FILE TO A FOLDER

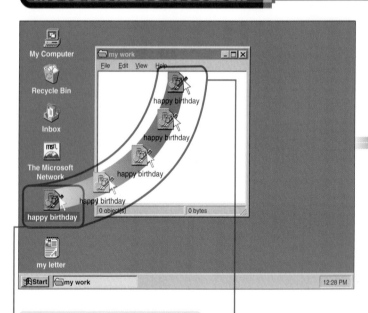

1 Position the mouse ⤢ over the file you want to move.

Note: To move more than one file, select the files. To select multiple files, refer to page 126.

2 Press and hold down the left button as you drag the mouse ⤢ to where you want to place the file.

132

You can reorganize the files stored on your computer by placing them in different folders.

Moving files is similar to rearranging documents in a filing cabinet to make them easier to find.

3 Release the button and the file moves to the new location.

COPY A FILE TO A FOLDER

To copy a file, perform steps **1** to **3**, except press and hold down Ctrl on your keyboard before and during step **3**.

(133)

COPY A FILE TO A FLOPPY DISK

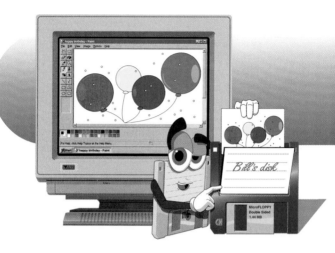

COPY A FILE TO A FLOPPY DISK

1 Insert a floppy disk into a drive.

You can make an exact copy of a file and then place the copy on a floppy disk.

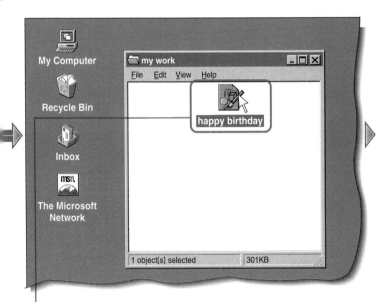

2 To select the file you want to copy, move the mouse ⤢ over the file and then press the left button.

Note: To copy more than one file, select the files. To select multiple files, refer to page 126.

CONTINUED

135

COPY A FILE TO A FLOPPY DISK

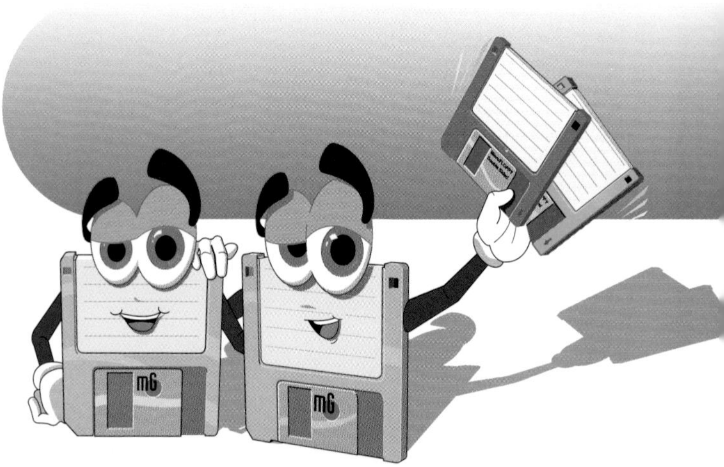

COPY FILE TO DISK (CONTINUED)

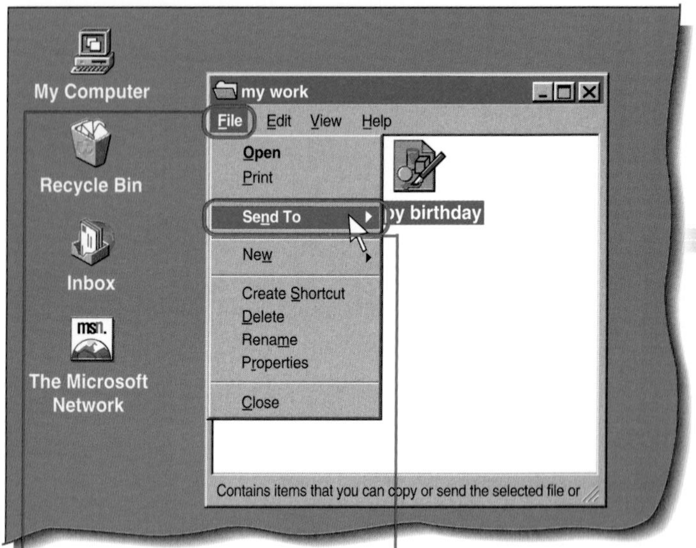
My Computer
Recycle Bin
Inbox
The Microsoft Network
my work
File
Edit
View
Help
Open
Print
Send To
New
Create Shortcut
Delete
Rename
Properties
Close
py birthday
Contains items that you can copy or send the selected file or

3 Move the mouse over **File** and then press the left button.

4 Move the mouse over **Send To**.

Copying a file to a floppy disk is useful if you want to give a copy of the file to a colleague.

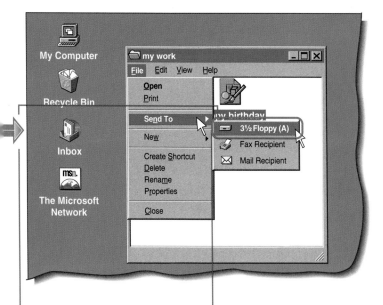

◆ This area lists the floppy drives on your computer.

5 Move the mouse ⇗ over the drive where you want to place a copy of the file and then press the left button.

RENAME A FILE

RENAME A FILE

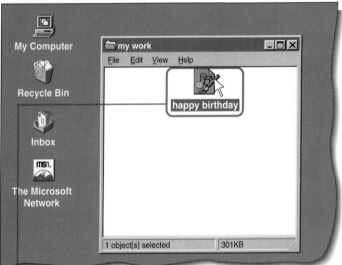

1 To select the file you want to rename, move the mouse ⌖ over the file and then press the left button.

You can give a file a new name to better describe its contents.

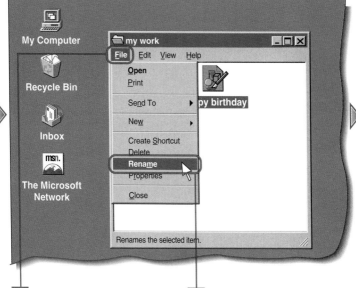

2 Move the mouse ⟍ over **File** and then press the left button.

3 Move the mouse ⟍ over **Rename** and then press the left button.

CONTINUED

RENAME A FILE

RENAME A FILE (CONTINUED)

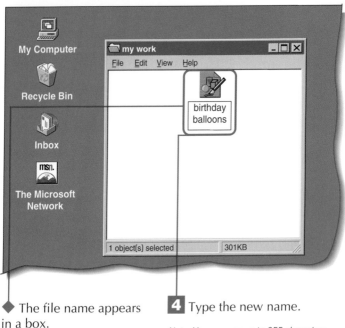

◆ The file name appears in a box.

4 Type the new name.

*Note: You can use up to 255 characters to name a file. The name cannot contain the characters \ ? : * " < > or |.*

Renaming a file
can make it easier
to find the file.

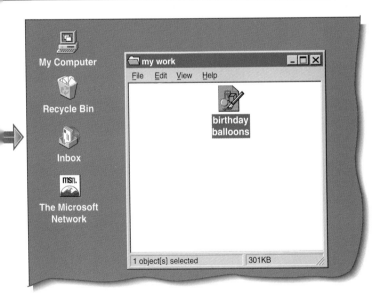

5 Press **Enter** on
your keyboard.

OPEN A FILE

You can open a file to display its contents on your screen. This lets you view and make changes to the file.

OPEN A FILE

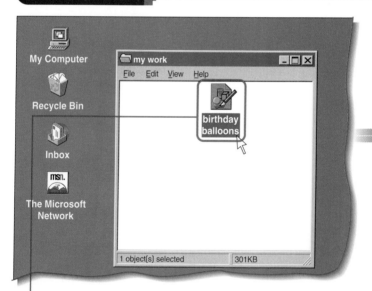

1 Move the mouse ⬦ over the file you want to open and then quickly press the left button twice.

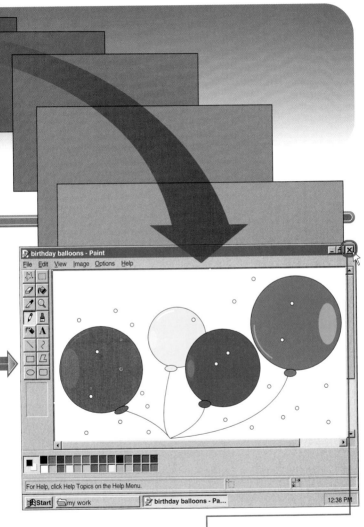

◆ The file opens. You can review and make changes to the file.

2 To close the file, move the mouse ↖ over ☒ and then press the left button.

143

OPEN A RECENTLY USED FILE

OPEN A RECENTLY USED FILE

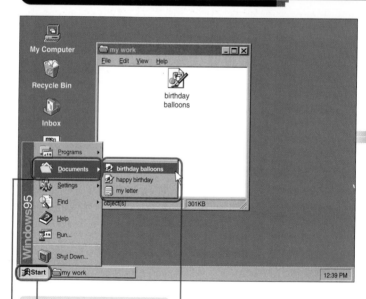

1 Move the mouse ↖ over **Start** and then press the left button.

2 Move the mouse ↖ over **Documents**.

◆ A list of the files you most recently used appears.

Note: Some files may not appear in this list.

3 Move the mouse ↖ over the file you want to open and then press the left button.

144

Windows remembers the files you most recently used. You can quickly open one of these files.

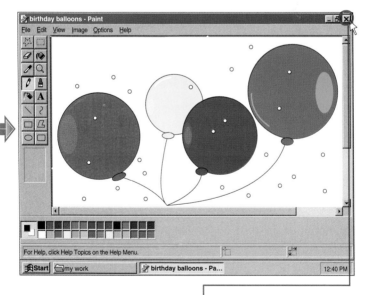

◆ The file opens. You can review and make changes to the file.

4 To close the file, move the mouse ⟋ over ☒ and then press the left button.

145

PRINT A FILE

PRINT A FILE

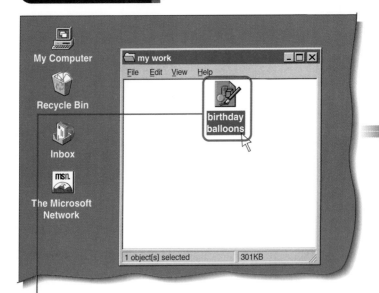

1 To select the file you want to print, move the mouse ⬚ over the file and then press the left button.

Note: To print more than one file, select the files. To select multiple files, refer to page 126.

You can produce a paper copy of a file stored on your computer.

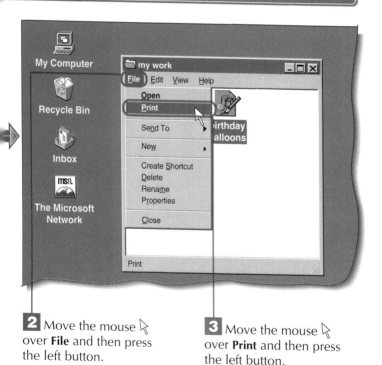

2 Move the mouse ⩗ over **File** and then press the left button.

3 Move the mouse ⩗ over **Print** and then press the left button.

DELETE A FILE

DELETE A FILE

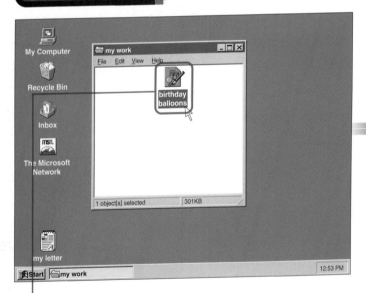

1 To select the file you want to delete, move the mouse ℞ over the file and then press the left button.

Note: To delete more than one file, select the files. To select multiple files, refer to page 126.

148

You can delete a file that you no longer need.

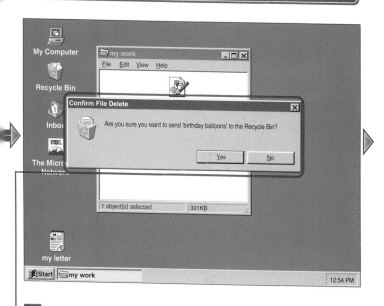

2 Press Delete on your keyboard and the **Confirm File Delete** dialog box appears.

CONTINUED

DELETE A FILE

DELETE A FILE (CONTINUED)

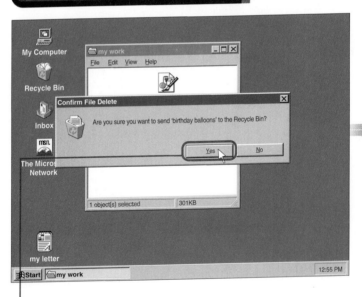

3 To delete the file, move the mouse ↕ over **Yes** and then press the left button.

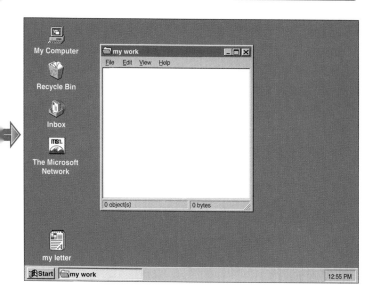

Make sure you do not delete files you may need in the future.

◆ The file disappears.

Note: To close a window, refer to page 42.

◆ If you delete a file you need, you can restore the file.

Note: For more information, refer to page 152.

RESTORE A DELETED FILE

RESTORE A DELETED FILE

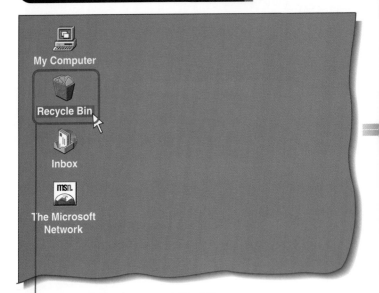

My Computer

Recycle Bin

Inbox

The Microsoft
Network

1 To display all the files you have deleted, move the mouse ⌖ over **Recycle Bin** and then quickly press the left button twice.

The Recycle Bin stores all the files you have deleted. You can easily restore any of these files.

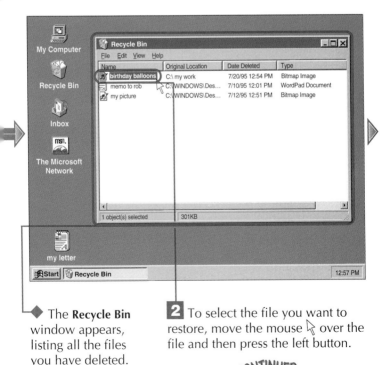

◆ The **Recycle Bin** window appears, listing all the files you have deleted.

2 To select the file you want to restore, move the mouse ℞ over the file and then press the left button.

CONTINUED

153

RESTORE A DELETED FILE

The appearance of the Recycle Bin indicates whether the bin contains deleted files.

RESTORE A DELETED FILE (CONTINUED)

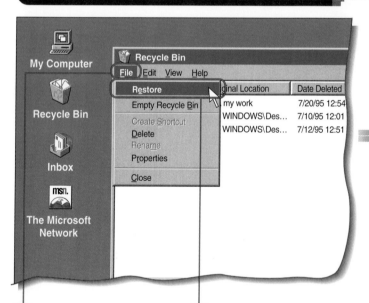

3 Move the mouse � over **File** and then press the left button.

4 Move the mouse � over **Restore** and then press the left button.

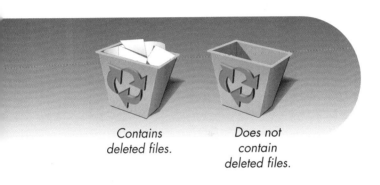

Contains
deleted files.

Does not
contain
deleted files.

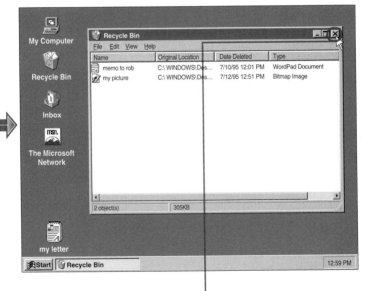

◆ The file disappears
from the list. Windows
places the file back in its
original location.

5 To close the **Recycle Bin**
window, move the mouse ⬚
over ⊠ and then press the
left button.

FIND A FILE

FIND A FILE

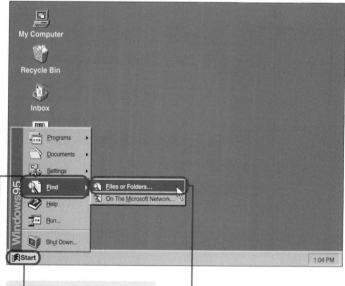

1 Move the mouse ⌖ over **Start** and then press the left button.

2 Move the mouse ⌖ over **Find**.

3 Move the mouse ⌖ over **Files or Folders** and then press the left button.

If you cannot remember the name or location of a file you want to work with, you can have Windows search for the file.

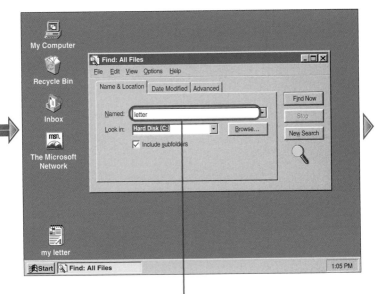

◆ The **Find: All Files** dialog box appears.

4 If you know all or part of the name of the file you want to find, type the name (example: **letter**).

CONTINUED

157

FIND A FILE

FIND A FILE (CONTINUED)

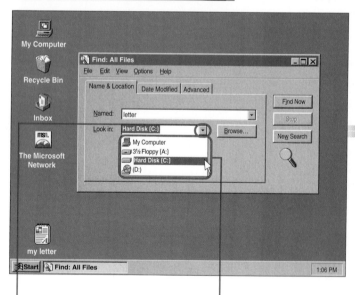

5 To specify where you want Windows to search for the file, move the mouse ↳ over ▾ in the **Look in:** box and then press the left button.

6 Move the mouse ↳ over the location you want to search and then press the left button.

158

You must specify the location you want Windows to search for the file.

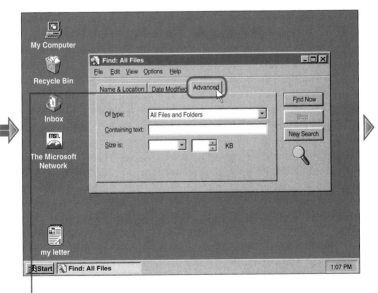

7 If you know a word or phrase in the file you want to find, move the mouse ⌖ over the **Advanced** tab and then press the left button.

Note: If you do not know a word or phrase in the file, skip to step 9.

FIND A FILE

FIND A FILE (CONTINUED)

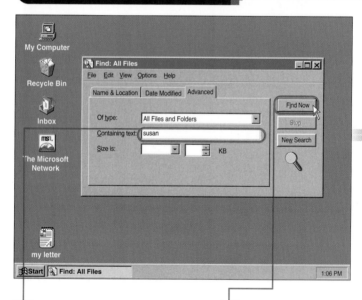

8 Move the mouse I over the box beside **Containing text:** and then press the left button. Type the word or phrase (example: **susan**).

9 To start the search, move the mouse ⤢ over **Find Now** and then press the left button.

When the search is complete, Windows displays a list of the files it found. You can open any of these files.

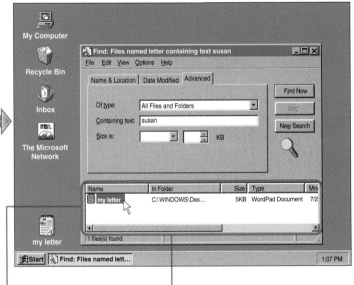

◆ This area displays the names of the files Windows found and information about each file.

10 To open a file, move the mouse ⬚ over the name of the file and then quickly press the left button twice.

Note: To close a window, move the mouse ⬚ over ✕ and then press the left button.

In this chapter you will learn how to customize the Windows screen to suit your needs. You will also learn how to change the date and the way the mouse works.

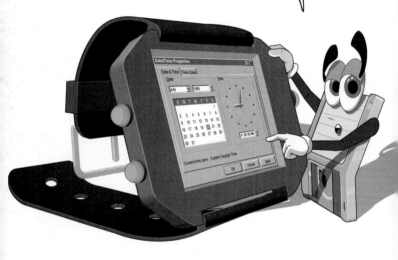

CHANGE WINDOWS SETTINGS

Change the Date and Time

Add Wallpaper

Change Screen Colors

Set Up a Screen Saver

Change Mouse Settings

CHANGE THE DATE AND TIME

CHANGE THE DATE AND TIME

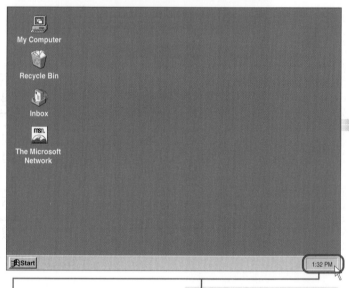

◆ This area displays the time set in your computer.

1 To change the date or time, move the mouse ⬉ over this area and then quickly press the left button twice.

You can easily change the date and time set in your computer.

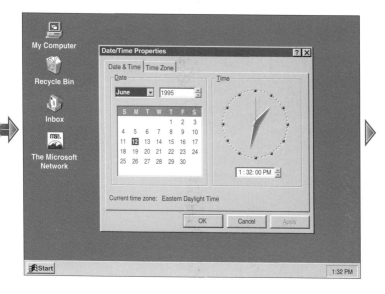

◆ The **Date/Time Properties** dialog box appears.

CONTINUED

CHANGE THE DATE AND TIME

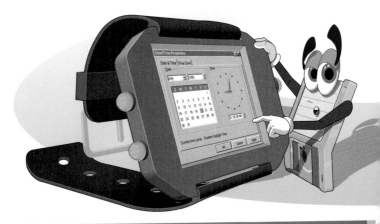

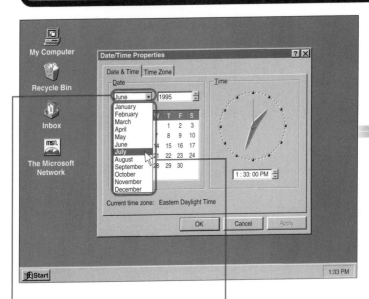

◆ This area displays the month set in your computer.

2 To change the month, move the mouse ▷ over this area and then press the left button.

3 Move the mouse ▷ over the correct month (example: **July**) and then press the left button.

166

It is important to have the correct date and time set in your computer. Windows uses this information to identify each document you create or update.

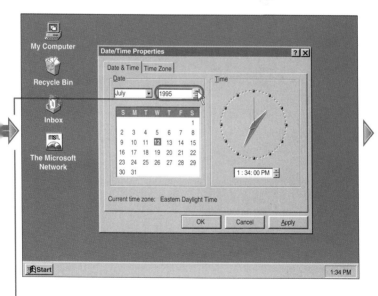

CONTINUED

◆ This area displays the year set in your computer.

4 To change the year, move the mouse ⟨ over ▼ or ▲ and then press the left button until the correct year appears (example: **1995**).

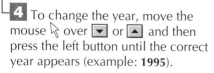

167

CHANGE THE DATE AND TIME

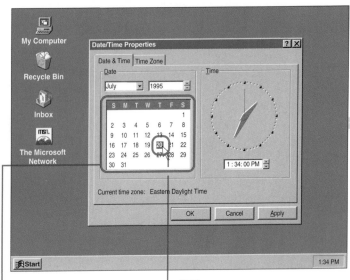

◆ This area displays the days in the month. The current day is highlighted.

5 To change the day, move the mouse ⌖ over the correct day (example: **20**) and then press the left button.

A computer has a built-in clock that keeps track of the date and time even when you turn off the computer.

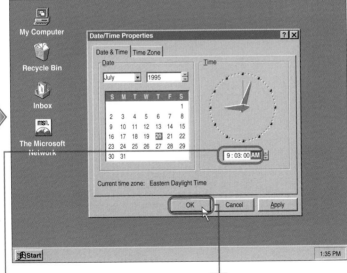

◆ This area displays the time set in your computer.

6 To change the time, move the mouse I over the part of the time you want to change and then quickly press the left button twice. Then type the correct information.

7 To apply the date and time changes you made, move the mouse over **OK** and then press the left button.

169

ADD WALLPAPER

ADD WALLPAPER

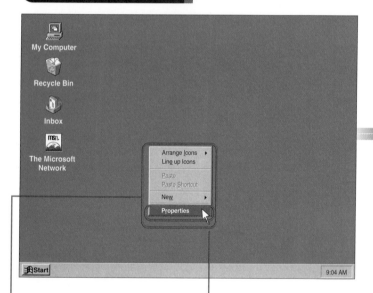

1 Move the mouse ⌖ over a blank area on your screen and then press the **right** button. A menu appears.

2 Move the mouse ⌖ over **Properties** and then press the left button.

◆ The **Display Properties** dialog box appears.

170

You can decorate your screen by adding wallpaper.

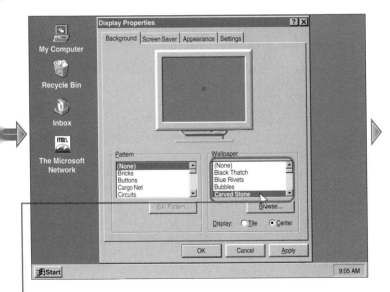

3 Move the mouse ⬚ over the wallpaper you want to display (example: **Carved Stone**) and then press the left button.

Note: To view all the available wallpapers, use the scroll bar. For more information, refer to page 50.

CONTINUED

ADD WALLPAPER

These are some of the wallpapers Windows offers.

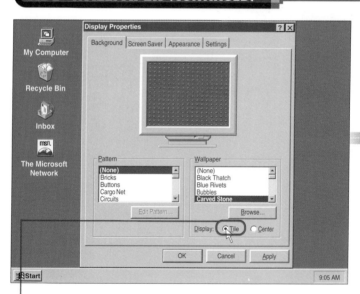

4 To cover your entire screen with the wallpaper you selected, move the mouse over **Tile** and then press the left button (O changes to ◉).

*Note: To place a small wallpaper image in the middle of your screen, select the **Center** option.*

172

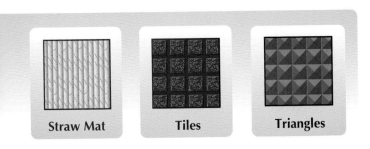

Straw Mat　　　**Tiles**　　　**Triangles**

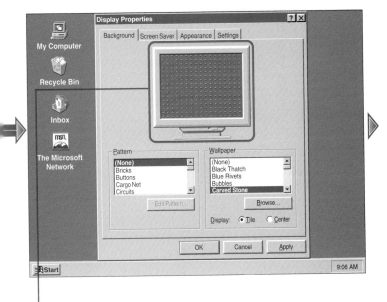

◆ This area displays
how the wallpaper you
selected will look on
your screen.

CONTINUED

ADD WALLPAPER

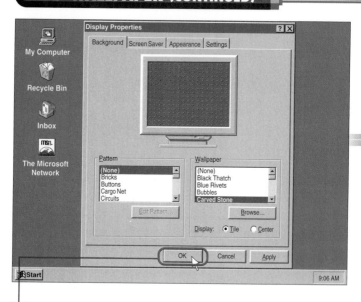

5 To display the wallpaper on your screen, move the mouse ⬚ over **OK** and then press the left button.

Adding wallpaper enhances the appearance of your screen.

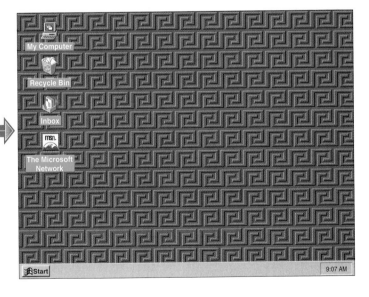

◆ Your screen displays the wallpaper you selected.

Note: To remove wallpaper from your screen, perform steps **1** to **3** starting on page 170, selecting **(None)** in step **3**. Then perform step **5**.

CHANGE SCREEN COLORS

CHANGE SCREEN COLORS

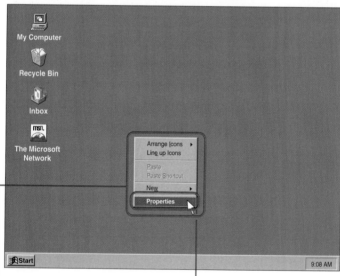

My Computer

Recycle Bin

Inbox

The Microsoft Network

| Arrange Icons ▸ |
| Line up Icons |
| Paste |
| Paste Shortcut |
| New ▸ |
| Properties |

Start

9:08 AM

1 Move the mouse ⟍ over a blank area on your screen and then press the **right** button. A menu appears.

2 Move the mouse ⟍ over **Properties** and then press the left button.

You can change the colors displayed on your screen to suit your preferences.

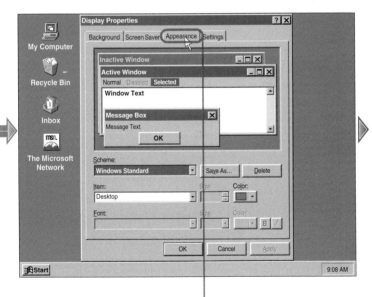

◆ The **Display Properties** dialog box appears.

3 Move the mouse ⬡ over the **Appearance** tab and then press the left button.

CONTINUED

177

CHANGE SCREEN COLORS

These are some of the color schemes Windows offers.

CHANGE SCREEN COLORS (CONTINUED)

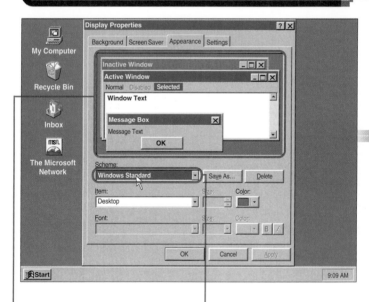

◆ This area displays the current color scheme.

4 To display a list of the available color schemes, move the mouse ⋈ over this area and then press the left button.

Wheat

Rose

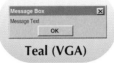

Teal (VGA)

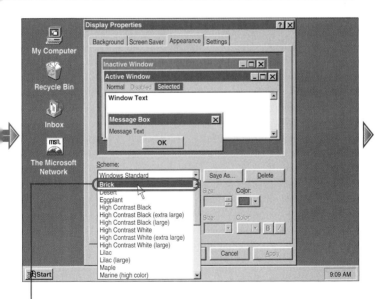

5 Move the mouse ⍩ over the color scheme you want to use (example: **Brick**) and then press the left button.

Note: To view all the available color schemes, use the scroll bar. For more information, refer to page 50.

CONTINUED

CHANGE SCREEN COLORS (CONTINUED)

◆ This area displays how your screen will look with the color scheme you selected.

6 To apply the color scheme, move the mouse over **OK** and then press the left button.

Changing your
screen colors enhances
the appearance of
your screen.

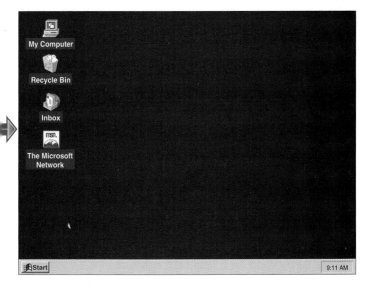

◆ Your screen displays
the color scheme you
selected.

*Note: To return to the original color
scheme, repeat steps* **1** *to* **6**
starting on page 176, selecting
Windows Standard *in step* **5** *.*

SET UP A SCREEN SAVER

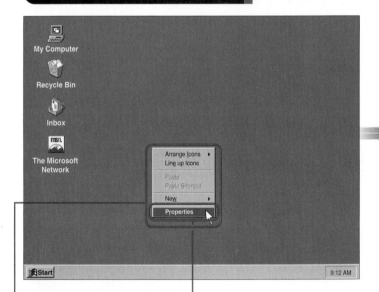

My Computer

Recycle Bin

Inbox

The Microsoft
Network

Arrange Icons ▶
Line up Icons

Paste
Paste Shortcut

New ▶

Properties

Start   9:12 AM

1 Move the mouse ⟍ over a blank area on your screen and then press the **right** button. A menu appears.

2 Move the mouse ⟍ over **Properties** and then press the left button.

182

A screen saver is a moving picture or pattern that appears on the screen when you do not use your computer for a period of time.

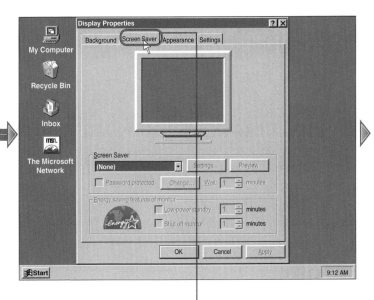

◆ The **Display Properties** dialog box appears.

3 Move the mouse ⌖ over the **Screen Saver** tab and then press the left button.

CONTINUED

SET UP A SCREEN SAVER

Screen savers were originally designed to prevent screen burn, which occurs when an image appears in a fixed position for a period of time.

SET UP A SCREEN SAVER (CONTINUED)

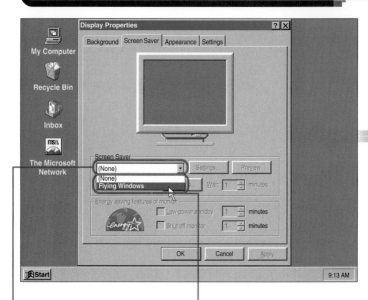

4 Move the mouse ⤢ over this area and then press the left button.

5 Move the mouse ⤢ over **Flying Windows** and then press the left button.

Note: You can buy sophisticated screen savers at most computer stores.

Today's monitors are better designed to prevent screen burn, but people still use screen savers for entertainment.

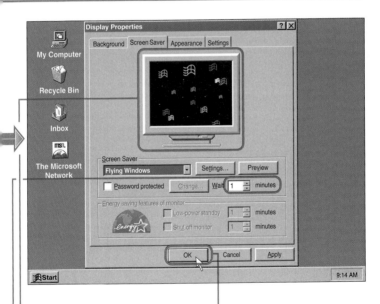

◆ This area displays how the screen saver will look on your screen.

◆ The screen saver will appear when you do not use your computer for the amount of time displayed in this area.

6 Move the mouse ⌖ over **OK** and then press the left button.

CHANGE MOUSE SETTINGS

CHANGE MOUSE SETTINGS

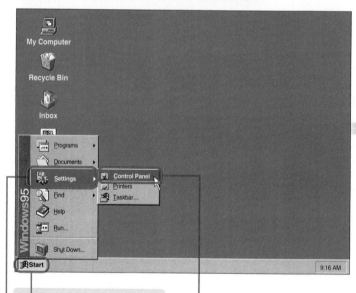

1 Move the mouse ⟍ over **Start** and then press the left button.

2 Move the mouse ⟍ over **Settings**.

3 Move the mouse ⟍ over **Control Panel** and then press the left button.

186

You can change the way your mouse works to suit your needs.

◆ The **Control Panel** window appears.

4 To change the mouse settings, move the mouse over **Mouse** and then quickly press the left button twice.

◆ The **Mouse Properties** dialog box appears.

CONTINUED

187

CHANGE MOUSE SETTINGS

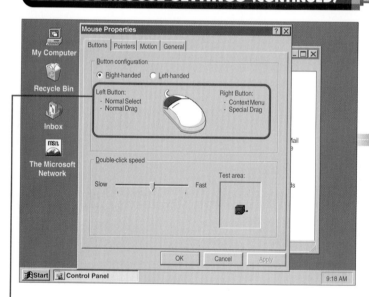

SWITCH BUTTONS

◆ This area describes the current functions of the left and right mouse buttons.

188

If you are
left-handed, you
can switch the functions
of the left and right mouse
buttons to make the
mouse easier
to use.

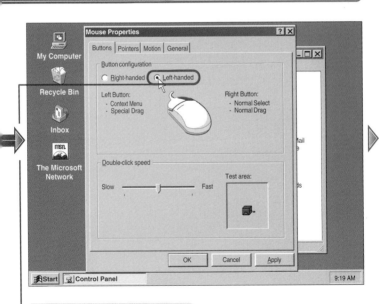

1 To switch the functions of the buttons, move the mouse ⌖ over this option and then press the left button (○ changes to ⦿).

Note: This change will not take effect until you confirm the changes. To do so, refer to page 193.

CONTINUED

189

CHANGE MOUSE SETTINGS

CHANGE MOUSE SETTINGS (CONTINUED)

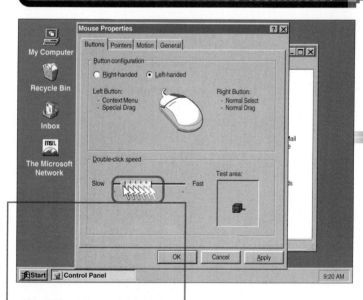

DOUBLE-CLICK SPEED

1 To change the double-click speed, move the mouse ▷ over ⬇.

2 Press and hold down the left button as you drag ⬇ to increase or decrease the double-click speed. Then release the button.

Note: If you are an inexperienced mouse user, you may find a slower speed easier to use.

You can change
the amount of time that
can pass between two clicks
of the mouse button for
Windows to recognize a
double-click.

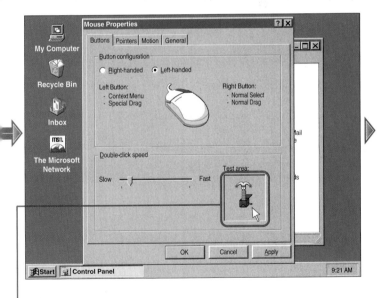

3 To test the double-click speed, move the mouse ↖ over this area and then quickly press the left button twice.

◆ The jack-in-the-box appears if you clicked at the correct speed.

Note: This change will not take effect until you confirm the changes. To do so, refer to page 193.

CONTINUED

CHANGE MOUSE SETTINGS

CHANGE MOUSE SETTINGS (CONTINUED)

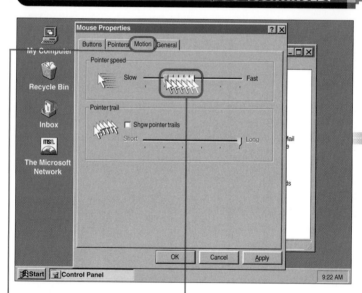

POINTER SPEED

1 Move the mouse ⩗ over the **Motion** tab and then press the left button.

2 To change the pointer speed, move the mouse ⩗ over ⬇.

3 Press and hold down the left button as you drag ⬇ to increase or decrease the pointer speed. Then release the button.

You can make
the mouse pointer
on your screen move
faster or slower.

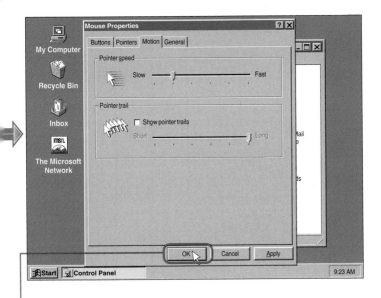

CONFIRM CHANGES

1 When you finish
selecting all the mouse
settings you want to change,
move the mouse ▷ over **OK**
and then press the left button.

MAINTAIN YOUR COMPUTER

Format a Disk

Detect and Repair Disk Errors

Defragment a Disk

FORMAT A DISK

FORMAT A DISK

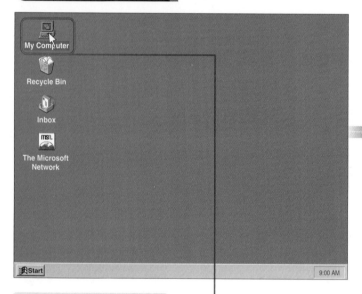

My Computer

Recycle Bin

Inbox

The Microsoft Network

Start · 9:00 AM

1 Insert the floppy disk you want to format into a drive.

2 Move the mouse ⌖ over **My Computer** and then quickly press the left button twice.

You must format a floppy disk before you can use it to store information.

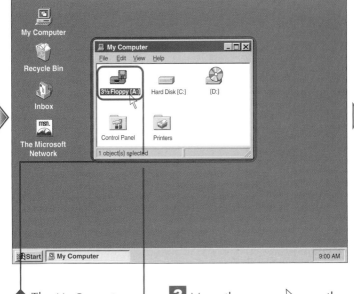

◆ The **My Computer** window appears.

3 Move the mouse ⌨ over the drive containing the floppy disk you want to format (example: **A:**) and then press the left button.

CONTINUED

FORMAT A DISK (CONTINUED)

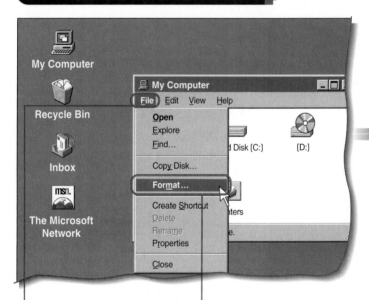

4 Move the mouse ⬚ over **File** and then press the left button.

5 Move the mouse ⬚ over **Format** and then press the left button.

◆ The **Format** dialog box appears.

Before formatting
a floppy disk, make sure
the disk does not contain
information you want to keep.
Formatting will remove
all the information on
the disk.

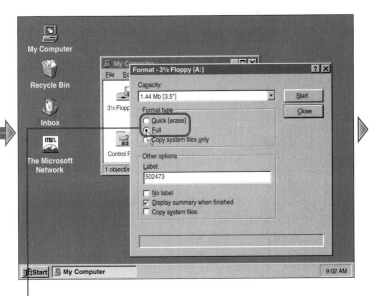

6 Move the mouse ⟍ over the type of format you want to perform and then press the left button (○ changes to ●). If the floppy disk has never been formatted, select the **Full** option.

Quick (erase)
Removes all files but does not scan the disk for damaged areas.
Full
Removes all files and scans the disk for damaged areas.

CONTINUED

199

FORMAT A DISK

When formatting a floppy disk, you must tell Windows how much information the disk can hold.

HIGH-DENSITY 1.44 Mb

A 3.5 inch floppy disk that has two holes and displays the HD symbol holds 1.44 Mb of information.

MicroFLOPPY
Double Sided
1.44 Mb

FORMAT A DISK (CONTINUED)

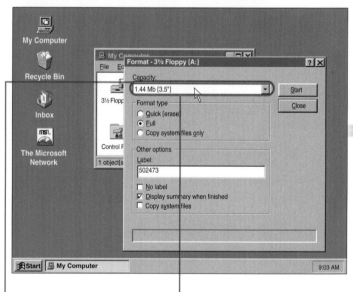

◆ This area displays how much information the floppy disk can hold.

7 To select a different capacity, move the mouse ⬚ over this area and then press the left button.

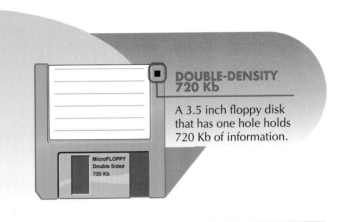

DOUBLE-DENSITY 720 Kb

A 3.5 inch floppy disk that has one hole holds 720 Kb of information.

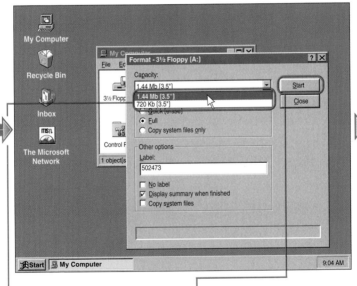

8 Move the mouse ⟋ over the capacity you want and then press the left button.

9 To start formatting the floppy disk, move the mouse ⟋ over **Start** and then press the left button.

CONTINUED

201

FORMAT A DISK (CONTINUED)

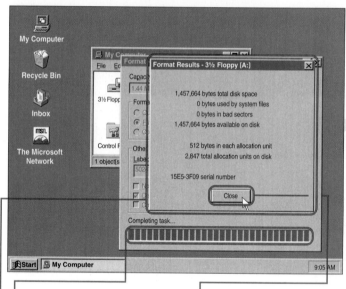

◆ This area displays the progress of the format.

◆ The **Format Results** dialog box appears when the format is complete. It displays information about the formatted disk.

10 To close this dialog box, move the mouse ⌖ over **Close** and then press the left button.

When the format is complete, you can use the disk to store information.

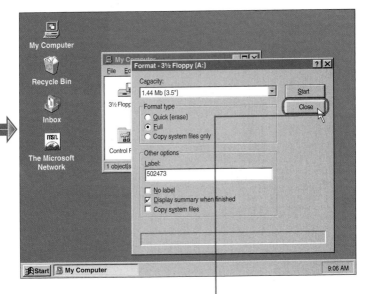

◆ To format another floppy disk, insert the disk and then repeat steps **6** to **10** starting on page 199.

11 To close the **Format** dialog box, move the mouse � over **Close** and then press the left button.

DETECT AND REPAIR DISK ERRORS

Hard Disk

DETECT AND REPAIR DISK ERRORS

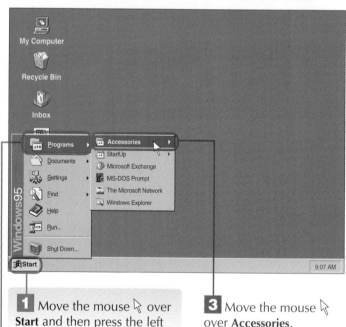

1 Move the mouse ⌖ over **Start** and then press the left button.

2 Move the mouse ⌖ over **Programs**.

3 Move the mouse ⌖ over **Accessories**.

You can improve the performance of your computer by using ScanDisk to search for and repair disk errors.

The hard disk is the primary device that a computer uses to store information.

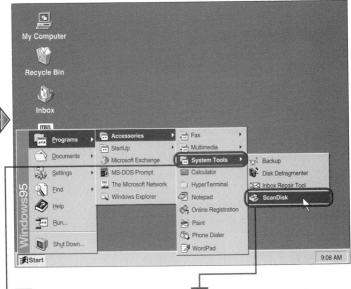

4 Move the mouse ⬚ over **System Tools**.

5 Move the mouse ⬚ over **ScanDisk** and then press the left button.

CONTINUED

DETECT AND REPAIR DISK ERRORS

DETECT AND REPAIR (CONTINUED)

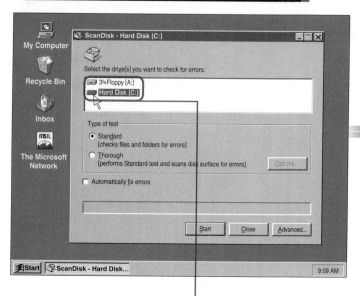

◆ The **ScanDisk** dialog box appears.

6 Move the mouse ⌖ over the drive you want to check for errors (example: **C:**) and then press the left button.

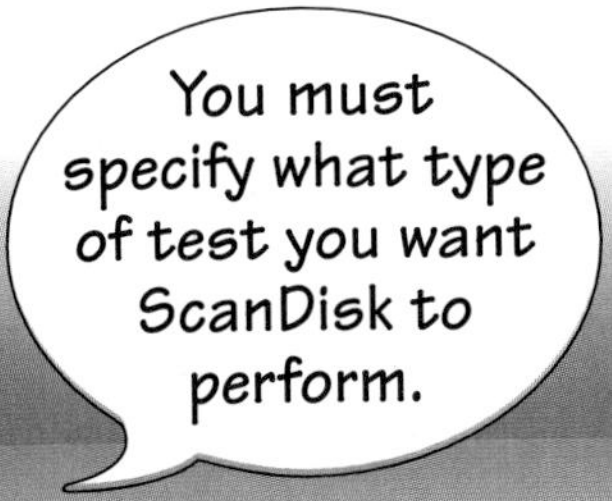
You must specify what type of test you want ScanDisk to perform.

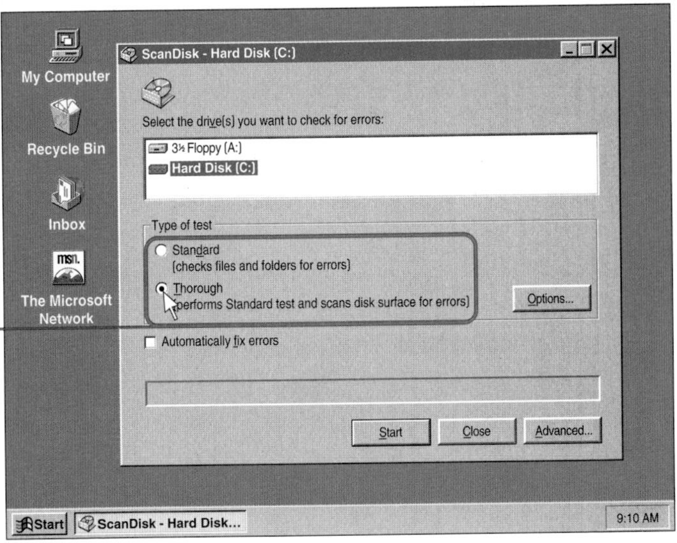
My Computer
Recycle Bin
Inbox
The Microsoft Network
ScanDisk - Hard Disk (C:)
Select the drive(s) you want to check for errors:
3½ Floppy (A:)
Hard Disk (C:)
Type of test
Standard
(checks files and folders for errors)
Thorough
(performs Standard test and scans disk surface for errors)
Options...
Automatically fix errors
Start
Close
Advanced...
Start
ScanDisk - Hard Disk...
9:10 AM

7 Move the mouse ↖ over the type of test you want to perform (example: **Thorough**) and then press the left button. ○ changes to ◉.

Standard
Checks files and folders for errors.

Thorough
Checks files, folders and the disk surface for errors.

CONTINUED

DETECT AND REPAIR DISK ERRORS

DETECT AND REPAIR (CONTINUED)

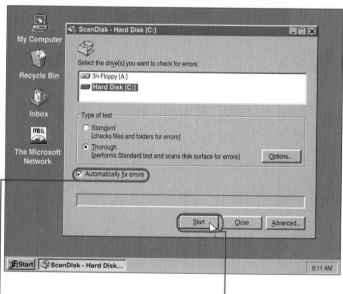

8 If you want Windows to automatically repair any disk errors it finds, move the mouse ⤳ over this option and then press the left button (☐ changes to ☑).

9 To start the check, move the mouse ⤳ over **Start** and then press the left button.

You can have Windows automatically repair any disk errors it finds.

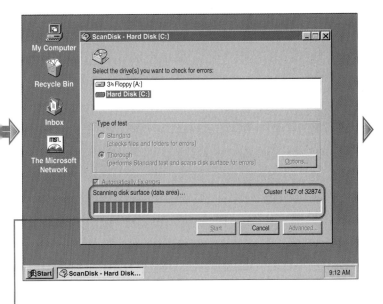

This area displays the progress of the check.

CONTINUED

DETECT AND REPAIR DISK ERRORS

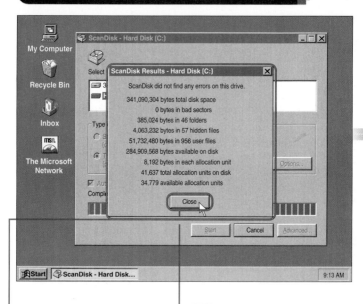

ScanDisk Results - Hard Disk (C:)

ScanDisk did not find any errors on this drive.

341,090,304 bytes total disk space
0 bytes in bad sectors
385,024 bytes in 46 folders
4,063,232 bytes in 57 hidden files
51,732,480 bytes in 956 user files
284,909,568 bytes available on disk
8,192 bytes in each allocation unit
41,637 total allocation units on disk
34,779 available allocation units

Close

◆ The **ScanDisk Results** dialog box appears when the check is complete. It displays information about the disk.

10 To close this dialog box, move the mouse ▷ over **Close** and then press the left button.

You should check your hard disk for errors at least once a month.

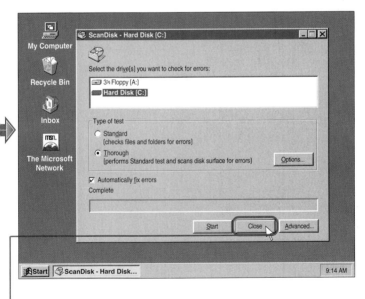

11 To close the **ScanDisk** dialog box, move the mouse ▷ over **Close** and then press the left button.

211

DEFRAGMENT A DISK

DEFRAGMENT A DISK

1 Move the mouse ⇖ over **Start** and then press the left button.

2 Move the mouse ⇖ over **Programs**.

3 Move the mouse ⇖ over **Accessories**.

You can improve the performance of your computer by using the Disk Defragmenter program.

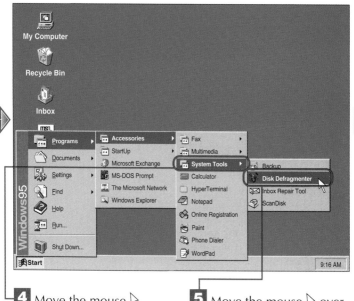

4 Move the mouse ⟍ over **System Tools**.

5 Move the mouse ⟍ over **Disk Defragmenter** and then press the left button.

CONTINUED

213

DEFRAGMENT A DISK

DEFRAGMENT A DISK (CONTINUED)

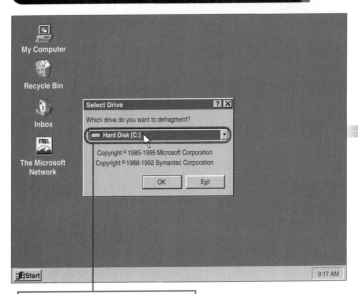

◆ This area displays the drive that Windows will defragment.

6 To select a different drive, move the mouse over this area and then press the left button.

214

The Disk Defragmenter program reorganizes the files stored on your hard disk. This reduces the time the computer will spend locating a file.

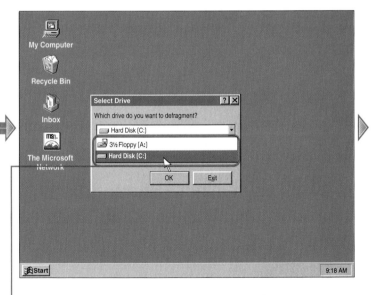

◆ A list of the drives on your computer appears.

7 Move the mouse ⌖ over the drive you want to defragment (example: **C:**) and then press the left button.

CONTINUED

215

DEFRAGMENT A DISK

DEFRAGMENT A DISK (CONTINUED)

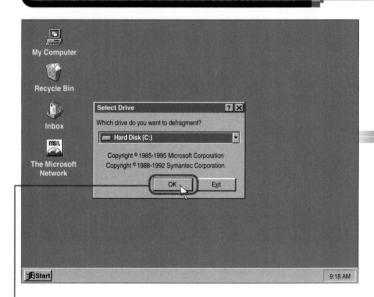

8 Move the mouse ⬚ over **OK** and then press the left button.

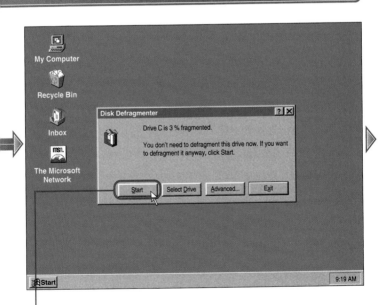

You can perform other tasks on your computer while Windows defragments a disk, but your computer will operate slower.

9 Move the mouse ⬡ over **Start** and then press the left button.

CONTINUED

DEFRAGMENT A DISK

DEFRAGMENT A DISK (CONTINUED)

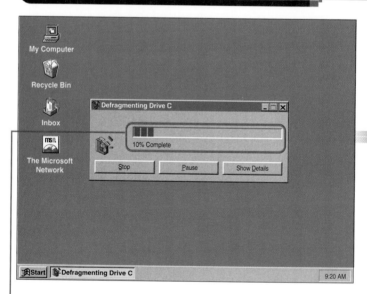

◆ This area displays the progress of the defragmentation.

You should defragment your hard disk at least once a month.

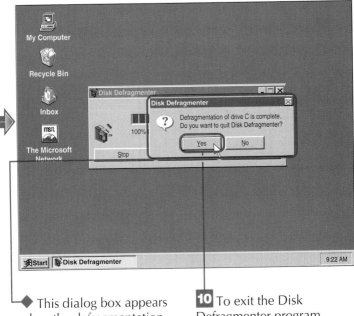

◆ This dialog box appears when the defragmentation is complete.

10 To exit the Disk Defragmenter program, move the mouse ▷ over **Yes** and then press the left button.

INDEX

INDEX